AGENDA

Hoofmarks issue

Dedication

This 'Hoofmarks' issue is dedicated
to Soulbury Solar Tropic (Troppie)
who died June 2007.

Also to a lover of horses, Emma
Cookson, now age 23, daughter of
William, the founding editor of *Agenda*

My Golden Horse

My golden horse, the night you were put down
I dreamt all the blue geraniums in the garden
had lost their heads, and the moon, not meant to be

full, was your exact colour: of a sun edged with red.
None of your blood shed, though, as it awoke me.

Before you, the May had dropped your silhouette,
its flowers like the last, long, winter-whitened hairs
you had just stepped out of as onto a summer prairie.

You were still a musical-box, with whinnies
of a counter-tenor for me, and shaped perfectly:

a mover even in your hopeless struggle to get up.
Worse than bramble tripwires constricted you
in the field's corner where you would never have lain,

your hindquarters suddenly gone, the silver of your shoes
miniature earth-crashed crescents sent to drain

the life from your veins. My golden horse, all the nights
to come without you, even the trees will lose their heads
and pave ground never to be pranced on by you again.

Your mare and I will know you are never properly gone,
your carats fretted into the fine gold-leaf of memory.

Patricia McCarthy

AGENDA

CONTENTS

Front cover: 'Lusitano under saddle', oil on paper by Leslie Medlock. Leslie grew up on the West Coast of Scotland and was pony-mad from a very early age. She had horses of her own, and her love of horses has remained a constant all her life. She has lived for several years in Paris and Brussels, and now resides in Mayfield, East Sussex. She runs a small art gallery, The Dark Horse, organises painting and sculpture classes there, and in her spare time she continues to paint and model in ceramics. www.thedarkhorsegallery.com.

Back cover: coloured collographs from 'The Garden of Earthly Delights' (artists book). Carolyn Trant, painter turned maker of artists books for nearly 20 years, has worked with poets such as Judith Kazentzis, David Harsent, Peter Abbs, and, now, with James Simpson whose work appears here. Her art books are in collections public and private across the UK, USA, Australia and Europe, including The British Library, V&A, National Art Library and The Tate. http://carolyntrantparvenu.blogspot.com

Editorial:

Help needed from every subscriber and contributor!

Many thanks to the Arts Council of England for giving *Agenda* a year's breathing space with another year's funding. Strict provisos, however, have to be adhered to now, in these economically difficult times, and alternative funding, along with an increase in the subscription list have to be found for next year in order to sustain *Agenda* as an ongoing, living poetic force and as a vital part of the national archive.

Many thanks, also, to Elizabeth Joyce Williams for here generous financial contribution.

Thanks, as always, too, to every reader, subscriber and contributor who make *Agenda* what it is.

*   *   *

And now for a plea to subscribers and contributors everywhere! Please don't forget to renew your subscriptions annually. Also, if **each one of you** could **find a friend** to give a subscription to and/or persuade a friend, or a library, or an institution such as a school or college, to subscribe, we will at least be starting to increase our subscription list.

A subscription to *Agenda* **as a Christmas present?** Why not?

Agenda's **first ever poetry competition:** make sure you enter and tell as many people you can about it.

Go on, get that friend now, and order those subscriptions as Christmas presents in good time to save you that Christmas rush!

Patricia McCarthy, Editor
Marcus Frederick, Administrator

7

Introduction

'A horse! a horse! my kingdom for a horse!'
                Shakespeare: *Richard III*

Welcome to this 'Hoofmarks' issue which contains, among other treasures, poems on horses, from many angles, by established, less known, as well as young poets, that I have been saving, waiting for the chance to include them in *Agenda*.

I used to tease the founding editor, William Cookson, about his predilection for oaks and creaking branches in poems. Any sign of one of those and, given that the poem was well-crafted and urgently written, it was well nigh always slipped in. I am guilty of the same: anything to do with a horse and I sit up carefully, grabbing onto the poem!

From time immemorial, horses have been important to man, appearing on cave drawings, frescoes, paintings, as sculptures, and in poems, not least in the bible, through the ages. They have served man, been his close companions, fought in war for him, carried heavy cargoes for him, pulled carriages, traps for tourists, given man endless pleasure, as well as a challenge to perfect what is probably the purest and most complex art of all: equitation. Remember Cleopatra's sigh 'O happy horse, to bear the weight of Antony!' Who can ever forget the sound of the horses in Erich Maria Remarque's *All Quiet on the Western Front* where the cry of wounded horses is 'the moaning of the world, it is the martyred creation, wild with anguish, filled with terror, and groaning'. It penetrates everywhere. Or Michael Longley's fine yet unbearably graphic 'Death of a Horse' (after Keith Douglas) that I cannot face quoting from here? Then, in Matthew Arnold's compelling narrative poem, 'Sohrab and Rustum', there is Ruksh, Rustum's 'brave steed' 'whose renown was noised through all the earth', who followed Rustum 'like a faithful hound at heel' and felt his master's pain as his own: 'from his dark compassionate eyes, /The big warm tears roll'd down, and caked the sand', recalling probably Homer's horses that demonstrated their mourning for Patroclus, their charioteer (as described in another of Michael Longley's powerful poems, 'The Horses').

Horses have always been my particular passion: all shapes and sizes – clothes-horses, rocking horses, glass horses. I will never forget the valiant cart-horses in the Ireland of my childhood years ago, overladen with coal, falling uphill and lying slumped, pinned beneath their shafts. The imaginary friend I had when very small owned a pony that clip-clopped up the lane so convincingly that everyone thought it was real. There was the piebald, Pinto, I used to borrow from the grocer's cart in Ireland, remove her blinkers and jump her over ditches and banks, even over unsuspecting lovers on occasions when they happened to be lying in the lea of a dry stone wall. The rotund, 40 year old Blue Cross-rescued Niggy, on loan for my sister, we didn't realise in those days hadn't been properly gelded. She would slide off backwards when he reared up on the back of every mare in sight. Then there was Sunny who went back and forth with me on the cattle boat across the Irish Sea about four times, for whom the policeman held up the traffic on Butt Bridge in Dublin as, like tinkers, we hacked her out to the suburbs through the docks; Sunny who jumped upturned boats along Killiney Strand, who jumped out of every field she was ever put in and had to be tracked down at midnights with a clothesline, in case a tinker's stallion got a hold of her. Sunny, that I always kept a tab on when I lived for many years abroad, and tried to buy back on my return, only to find she had been put down because her heart had gone. More recently, Pom, a chestnut Arab I rescued, with legs like matchsticks, Troppie a magical palomino with a devilish streak whose feet hardly touched the ground, owned by me for eighteen years until he died aged thirty in the field three years ago; Polka, my little bay mare, also rescued, my soul mate, whom I have had for twenty four years, now twenty-eight, very agile still; and Dolly, a big grey thoroughbred mare of twenty-two, bred as a race-horse, a national sidesaddle champion whom I was given last year as a friend for Polka (otherwise she was going to be put down) as her owner sadly had died. Dolly and Polka who walk together in synchronisation like stately, often frisky, matrons; drink at the same time from the water trough; eat grass nose to nose. Lucky I am to have them alive still, but for how much longer?

I hope, therefore, that I will be forgiven my slight indulgence this time, and that readers will enjoy the variety of poems, horsey and otherwise, the essays and reviews.

What better note to end on than a quotation from Yeats' 'At Galway Races':

> We'll learn that sleeping is not death,
> Hearing the whole earth change its tune,
> Its flesh being wild, and it again
> Crying aloud as the racecourse is,
> And we find hearteners among men
> That ride upon horses.

Here is a wish, then, for all the readers and writers involved in this issue of *Agenda* to be those very 'hearteners', whatever horses they ride: be they real, those of the sea, of the wind, or of Pegasus, from whose hoofmarks spring lines of inspired poetry.

Patricia McCarthy

9

Kate Woodyatt: 'Lady Godiva', egg tempora and oil on canvas
(Kate Woodyatt's painting 'Odysseus and the Sirens' was on the front cover
of *Agenda*, Vol. 40, No.4, the 'Translation as Metamorphosis' issue).

Andrew McNeillie

The Far Moss

The location of the far moss
beyond finding now, a mystery
as remote the day
the runaway pony
held the high ground
trotting off warily
on the skyline
keeping well ahead
as they sought him
cursing the god-given day.

While the others cut peat
and the sky peeped
into new puddles of blue
and the peewits scolded
the sandpiper piped
of winter shoreland
the grouse cackled
the harrier hunted
the curlew lamented
moorland life.

And the cart alone
praised the Lord, its shafts
upraised, free of burden,
a triumph of equine rebellion
to remember at the hearth
in soporific peatsmoke
laced with drink
the day the pony
ran them ragged
and the beauty there.

O the far moss!
Its location a mystery now
in square miles of forestry
though not so far away
in time found here
as if preserved in peat
awaiting re-discovery
or re-emergence
of heather-bell and
Adam's vine and sheep.

Christopher Locke

Red Horse

San Miguel de Allende, Mexico

The colour of beef sliced
to its blue, the sky
frames adobe mansions
too expensive to house
taste. Broken bottles embed
the tops of their high walls
like a glassblower's dream
of revenge. The bronchial
mesh of mesquite trees stiffen
the air, and birdsong unplugs
its numerous fountains under
this blue of tight hours, of heat
translucent in its heavy broth
of light. Until at last, up the
cobbled street, a lone girl pulls
a small red horse on tin wheels
so as to make the shadows
ring with her love.

Lyn Moir

Gansu Flying Horse 1

Curled feather
on eggshell
his hoof touches
the swallow's neck

they soar
bronze to lapis
gravity suspended.

If the swallow
can carry him
he will support
the universe
on the tip
of his twisted tail.

Gansu Flying Horse 2

'Call it a training flight,'
the swallow said,
fluttering wings.

Touching the bird's back
the horse's hoof
felt hollow bones, withdrew.

'Don't mind me: I'm
strong as the wind,
fast as the sun.'

'The other way round, surely?'
'Whatever,' the bird muttered
as the horse flexed,

a ballet dancer
touching silver shoe
to shining feathers.

'Chocks away!' The swallow soared,
wheeling above the pagodas.
'We must make a dragon of you

by order of Emperor Wu.' Sighing,
the horse raised his head,
mane a banner in the wind.

Majestically, the two flew west
over Mingsha mountain,
circled the Crescent Lake,

terrifying peasants and merchants,
camels and cameleers.
'Quite exhilarating, this,

but I was promised wings.'
'And wings you have, mine. This way
those dots below see you, flying

as if you were born to it. I
am invisible.' The swallow preened.
'Makes you look supernatural.'

Entranced, the horse pirouetted,
lashed his tail, pawed the air
with three free hooves.

'Steady on, it won't look good
if you crash to earth. This
is a propaganda exercise.

Emperor Wu must be seen
to have the most advanced
military technology. You.

With your magical flight, no foe
can resist the Son of Heaven.
You, and I with you... immortal.

Don't panic, horse, steady boy –
Wuwei tower, Wuwei tower,
swallow to control, coming in to land.'

Thomas O'Grady

Magritte

This morning,
sunlight streaming in shafts
  past the bedroom blinds –

too bright . . . too early – my mind
  drifted back between
those slanted slats to a steamy

  labyrinth of sheets
and last night's dream of a high-stepping
  stallion bridled, saddled,

straddled, steered through that glowing
  grove in Magritte's
Le blanc-seing . . . a thinned-out

  first-growth stand
of sturdy oak just turning leaf. The story
  of the autumn of my life?

O that well-heeled damsel – hand in glove,
  reins at the ready, crop
by her thigh – dressed for dressage.

  Piaffe! Passage!

Note: 'Le blanc-seing' is the name of the painting of a horse by Magritte

17

Angela France

Empty Horses

They line up around the towns;
dark faces hang over fences,
gates, stable doors.

They don't turn away.
Grass grows.

They flick at flies,
shuffle, jostle a little.
Stay.

People stop looking, drivers
keep eyes ahead, windows
on trains and buses blinded
by newspapers, coats, bags.

Buddleia sprouts
in petrol stations. Badgers play
on motorways. Verges widen.

The horses toss their heads
at changing weather,
blow gently, don't whicker
or whinny.

They stay in line,
creak light from their joints
as they stamp, swish tails.

Alison Brackenbury

Exmoor

The moment when we saw the foal
was past the scramble to the cairn
where the young clambered over stones
with new shoes, supple, fragile bones,
before you lay down, caught by pain,
for those skies stripped us to the soul.

A stray mare led us to the foal.
Huge-bellied, she had wandered off.
It lay below the flow of wind.
Thick-maned, its mother stood behind,
her head down, dreaming still of wolf.
It slept where heathers rode and fell.

Its muzzle gleamed like flour on coal.
It twitched a tasselled tail at flies.
But we moved on, with stubborn feet,
down Iron Age banks, to tarmac's heat.
Though I have lost that ache, those skies,
I float on heather with the foal.

Laminitis

Sick at heart, not as sick as the pony
Hobbling on her hind feet, I lead her in.
Rich grass seethes in her blood. She cannot be
At ease, shifts, flexes fetlocks, stares at me.

Here is the bucket with the drug's stirred white.
Will she always be lame? No time to think.
Let her lick all; say, as a parent might
'In twenty minutes you will be all right.'

Kick down the crumbled shavings of her bed,
A softer chill beneath her burning feet.
Brush off her scurf and dust. The watch hands speed,
Her fidgeting grows slow. She drops her head,

She chews, as horses do, relaxed, at peace,
Sinks down her quarters, sags each glossy knee,
White with wood-dust, back legs stretch stiff and straight.
Weightless, half-closed, her eye stays fixed on me.

John Wesley's Horse

Riding from Durham to Devon,
he preached an animal heaven.
Wesley said happiness would suit
part of creation labelled 'Brute',

'without alloy or interruption'.
No cat flaps, bridles, sales' commotion.
The beaten horse, the tortured dog
were not shut out by Wesley's God

but promised loudly 'without end',
their meadows, mice and biscuit blend.
Riding from barn door to beach
John Wesley practised what he preached.

Though horses were tight-reined in town
he let his own stretch its neck down,
to snatch, on clifftops, clover, thyme,
frail rose and tooth-brown dandelion.

John Wesley, I face deeper night.
I stare into the same blind light.
I wish you, in the empty hearse
Your horse's heaven. You could do worse.

Fred Beake

The Stable

Then the house built for them was still raw and barely lived in,
      though the leaves of the ancient trees were gold in their autumn.

The back path to the stable she had insisted on
      was barely the diameter of the skirts that cumbered her.

The pony at least could be got along it after each use
      but the trap always scraped its varnish

and this was before the stone was covered in verdigris
      or the nettles resumed their nature

and detritus was bound to accumulate eventually
      (though the workmen had striven).

Anyhow, he knew future dwellers here would curse his love
      because she had desired a stable

where there was no room. But he loved her mouth,
      though he knew her beyond prediction

comparing her to a black squall line on a sapphire ocean
      from which dark hounds would burst into Heaven.

Fawzia Kane

Carnevale

San Marco can be so banal
at this time of year. We repaint our skins,
tighten our masks, until the gaps
in our eyes begin to show so little,
even nothing, sometimes. Our fingers
can only point, fan out, embroider
our tired songs. We bind our smiles
with nets of silk, they hold our sighs
just over the oily stink
of this water's edge; while from afar,
among that drumbeat sound of hooves
on stone, our blood-coloured shrouds are borne
above the crowds, unfurled from poles,
floating, slowly, ever closer.

Joseph Allen

Black Horses

The house is unusually quiet,
strange to see father
on a work day,
idle hands fidgeting
with his best collar.

Neighbours come and go,
woman fuss over
plates of sandwiches,
occasionally a comforting hand
descends on my head in passing.

Two great black horses
seem to fill the street,
breaths vaporised in the air.

Housewives stand guard
on their doorsteps,
arms crossed upon aproned breasts.

As the cortège makes its way
along the road
I am led indoors
to a house
that has changed forever.

Wendy Holborow

Dead Horses

The razor sun scrapes the sand
where the dead horse sinks
like the carcass of a wrecked ship.
Desert dogs shelter in the shade
of the cave of his skull –
they have picked him clean.

The second horse
dead a day or two,
legs stiff and straight.
His death so public.
No pyramid grave for him
just the great waves of sand
and the fearsome sun.

I thought I saw him tremble –
the membrane of his eyes moved,
the dogs already eating a trail
to their new cave.

Ridden hard
by men with shipwrecked minds
who scuttle souls,

the diabolical howl
was me, crying black tears
as the sand ached yellow.

John Freeman

Being Read

For Kerry Hardie

Like a horse standing day and night
in the clean loneliness of the field
among the sounds the wind lifts up,
aware slowly of a consciousness
close-by, is a two-legged thing
with eyes, looking the horse over
for a long time, appraising
the curving mane's dips and rises,
a poised hoof resting at a tilt.
Even praise is intrusive.
Leave the wild spirit its unselfconsciousness.
It is fathomless. Would you finger God's beard?
Not enough to be admirer, well-wisher.

Kathy Miles

Travelling Fair

A plastic bag gusts against your cheek
like a wraith. In the dust, blown papers,
greasy with chips and onions. Hot dogs
coned into tissue. Oily smoke, smell of diesel,
the growl of engines grinding to a halt.

Spangles on the big steel arms of the Ali Baba
and Super Star. The carousel, whirling its circle
of scarlet horses. In the dark spindle of rain
children are swirled like spoons in teacups,
the Ferris Wheel a high arc in the sky.

Mirrors, where you can be thin as a whip
or fat as a macaroon. Hooking yellow ducks
with a small loop, trying your luck on the rifle range.
Stalls of clothes and Christmas cards,
hooped earrings gleaming in the drift of steam.

How do they fold up the Twister? Do they pack
the legs of the Orbiter, like an iron spider
into trucks and lorries, breath expiring from its joints?
Are the horses stabled in pantechnicons?
Or do they gallop the night, wooden manes streaming
out in the freedom of evening air,
dreaming of fields of candy floss, toffee apple treats?

David Cooke

Work Horses

The clanking compound of the old Simmonds
brewery, where my dad did casual shifts
at times that work was slack on the buildings,
is buried now somewhere beneath the graceless
panels of the multi-storey car park
and the chat that drifts across
from the cappuccino pavement.

Born to a scant inheritance of rushy Sligo acres,
my dad was bred like his brothers
to follow the work, sending remittances home
from London, Reading, and Philadelphia –
for worklessness
would have been their defining shame.

And somewhere, too, in the grainy hinterland
of just remembered childhood
I am watching a drayman
as he guides heraldic, towering horses
through a time-thinned stream of traffic.
Their sinews barely tensed,
they go unfussed about their business.

Krupskaya

When I answered the letters Ulyanov
wrote me, I had guessed already
what love might mean: my attentiveness
a discipline to make me as pure
as our shared white exile,
our sweet talk sinking
into the language of a big idea.

The exhilaration. Like a troika ride
through candied forest –
the abruptly shaken manes of horses
scattering their halo of sound
until we are distant,
disappearing, reduced at last
to a quietness wrapped in tinsel.

And such contentment in possessing
only what we needed: our books, ourselves,
a purpose. Years later we visited
terraced slums, and then worked on
into a foreign night –
our homeless script like figures
tramping across the snow.

Lucinda Carey

Out of Bracken

Chestnut horses breast the forest's bracken,
And silver glints the metal armour as birch trees,
They arise and advance from the galloping
Swiftness of morning mist when Apollo lifts the reins.

Iron shod hooves thudding, the snickering of bits.
Stirrups, leather and black manes rising and falling
And the splattering of mud droplets in arcs,
From the infrequent boggy greenways of Ashurst.

Then silence, except for an axe stroke afar
And two squirrels chasing about the treetops.

Katherine Dimma

More True

A knife broke into my house, splitting it open –
sunlight's dark horses decanted.
Devils and angels flew up into the air –
their spirit wings hard to distinguish.

All the while I'd been slicing holes in your roof.

My house collapsed –
    in there, the faith was more true.

Felix Dennis

I Bit the Hand that Fed Me

I bit the hand that fed me,
And bled it in my grip,
The left was held in friendship –
His right concealed a whip.

The faithless fool still curses,
He calls us dogs and curs,
But I have learned from horses –
Too many men love spurs.

Andrew McNeillie

'Word Shod'

'Neptune tapped a rock and up sprang a horse. I saw the sea and my heart rode away. So it rides now at the drop of a hat, not for escape, but for respite'.

Once by Andrew McNeillie

P. McCarthy: It could be said that you, of all poets, do not need to be interviewed because you have written so articulately, generously and searchingly about your own early life in two Memoirs, *Once* and *An Aran Keening*, revealing the seeds of the person you have become today as both man and writer. Do you intend to follow these memoirs with sequels up to the present day?

Andrew McNeillie: Well, I am writing something I'm calling *In the Midst of Life*. I don't know about seeing it published. I'm doing it for my family, my daughter and son, I mean; for my grand-children when I am gone and my ashes disposed three ways, on the hill at North Clutag where my brother and I 'watered in' my father's ashes with Bladnoch whisky; in the far corner eastwards at Dulyn, where the stream tumbles from the six-hundred-foot crag and feeds into a little bay, in eastern Snowdonia; and along the tidemark at Cill Mhuirbhigh, if they won't admit me to the *cimetière marin* there. I hope to make my family laugh by my story. I take my cue from Les Murray. He has a little poem that adapts the English *Book of Common Prayer* to read: 'In the midst of life we are in employment.' I would say this has always been an article of faith with me but ne'er so well expressed as by Les. So this will be my life in employment. I'm writing it in a more garrulous free-running style than is usual for me. In my earlier passages of employment as a news reporter, I had some rum times. Since then, I have had what many in academe would consider a successful career in academic publishing. I think I did make a difference in my line of business. But I never sought or pursued any such thing as a career. It fell out that way. My priority has always been to get by and to preserve myself, my own agenda. (If I may make free with that word in these pages.) I have always been a bit delinquent and stolen what slice of time I could from employers, while meeting or exceeding their 'targets'. I haven't much time for the managerial classes, the career monkeys, with or without MBAs. Taken all in all, they seem thick-necked desperadoes to me, and, as Hopkins said in a different context, 'their packs infest the age'. My difficulty is that I love to work but hate employment. Work is to employment as heaven is to hell, to my mind. I love to work and am always at it. Income is the snake in the grass. I've always scotched it the best I could. I also love physical work. Set me digging and I'll dig all day. I'm not a new age person, far from it. I dig in memory of my father and my peasant forebears, like my Aunt Mary who might demand to know of all this in *Agenda*, 'For any sake, could you not hold less noise?'

P. McC: Talking of Memoirs, your prose seems to be part of your whole poetic process, linking you to the prose-poetry of Joyce, Jean Genet, Proust, Djuna Barnes. Is this deliberate?

A. McN: I have written one work I respect unreservedly, *An Aran Keening* – while I do recognize its failings, or shortcomings. It also bears inspection where to my mind inspection matters, among the people of Inis Mór, for it makes free with their recent past, and they'd be justified in vilifying me. But they don't. I was little more than a youth and a green fool at the time, but even most readers tell me they love the writing. If only they knew how much I love them and respect them for bearing all they have to bear, the world wrested from them in the name of history and heritage. I've come to know a broad spectrum of people on the island since those days of my young manhood. They're the best community of people I know outside my own family in Little Ireland (in the Machars of Wigtownshire). The Irish have applauded my book to the same degree that English metropolitans have never given it a second glance if they've ever seen it. That my prose is poetic – if my prose is poetic (the word must be earned) – it owes nothing I can trace to literary modernism, except more recently to David Jones. (I mean, I did deliberately consider his example when writing the middle section 'The Black Lake' to my book *Once*.) That is, consciously. When I was nineteen, I had already read *Ulysses* – in a fortnight on the Shropshire Union Canal, on a trip with my first girlfriend. I grew up in a house in which extremely good prose was written almost every day of the week, where a story-telling tradition out of the Machars of Wigtownshire lived in the tenor of my father's voice. He was one of that extraordinary breed we don't have now in the desperate age of 'Creative Writing', of autodidact compulsive writers. He worked in a factory all the time I was at home, and published over forty books (one or two yet to be got out of print, some soon to be brought back), radical novels in his early years, one filmed in Wicklow with Abbey and Gate Theatre Players, by Paul Rotha. That is, I had all this wired into me from birth. My father wrote his novel *No Resting Place* about traveller people under the direct influence of J. M. Synge, but also out of personal experience among the people of the Machars and the travellers there, the Kyles and the Irvines. He completed it in the six weeks before I was born. The movie went to the Venice film festival. My father never wrote verse, but his writing is full of poetic flight and flights. This was definitive for me, enabling and disabling, as you can imagine. May I add, however, that I love Genet and he has entered a poem of mine, indirectly; and when I was working near Liverpool as a new reporter and living in a condemned 'sea-captain's house' at Waterloo, where a whore operated in the room opposite mine, I did read and was fascinated by *Nightwood*. I also read *At-Swim-Two-Birds* and discovered Flann O'Brien. But these didn't get into my bloodstream there and then, Proust would be the one to learn from, as Tim Robinson has done so masterfully.

P. McC: How much fiction do you consider does come into play when looking back, as you do, in *Once*, 'from the vantage and disadvantage point of sixty years'?

A.McN: Don't we all know memory is one of the least reliable things we have? Yet we stake everything by it. (Think of the courts of law and witness.) There's less fictionalising in *Once* – which I'm proud to say my brother, sister and mother applaud (we scattered my father's ashes before he could read it) – than in *An Aran Keening*. That's an altogether more sophisticated piece of work, playing with all manner of perspectives and modes. When my father read it, his first remark to me was to wonder at how 'honest' I had been. (As you know he is represented in its pages, very crucially.) And indeed I had been deliberately 'honest'. But there is honesty and honesty in writing. A just representation never suffered for a little raw truth. Raw truth's a Trojan horse with invention in its belly, like Jonah in the whale. If I had a greater mind I would write fiction. Which is one way of saying that great art ventriloquises. Shakespeare is all ventriloquy, is he not?

P. McC: As a self-avowed shy man, you are surprisingly and analytically revealing of yourself in your Memoirs. Can the same be said of the main body of your poetry where you seem always intent on the 'story'. Or is it more complex here, and you are intent upon keeping the reader 'wondering/ what it is you're up to, haunting the page at/ the edge of sense' as you posit in your collection, *Slower* (Carcanet, 2006)?

A. McN: I used to be painfully shy in my youth and early manhood. But I'm not so shy now. I think I am as you say 'revealing' in my prose, but the Trojan horse principle is also involved in that. If you manage to seem 'surprisingly and analytically revealing' (even to be so, as I hope I also am), you can slip in other dimensions of meaning the more easily. I know I employed such strategies very deliberately in the Aran memoir. Not that I claim to know what I was doing in writing that book. These things are part of a dynamic that controls you as much as you control it. There's no doubt that the poem affords a different opportunity, a different route to come at things, than prose, even highly poeticised, inflected prose allows. I'm pleased to think I might seem more intent on the 'story' in my attempts at poems. I do know that the poem ought to be more complex and even more simple. I think when I wrote those lines you quote from the 'Glyn Dŵr Sonnets' I was urging a corrective to myself, to aspire to work more at 'the edge of sense'. Though I didn't know it then, I think I had in mind something like Douglas Dunn's expression regarding the 'no-place' of art. I think I recognized that I needed another dimension and I tried to provide it in the next book of poems.

P. McC: The business of the 'self' or the 'I' in poetry: I notice in *Slower*, at times you are the conscious poet e.g. in 'Meditation on Armistice Day', you refer to a 'rackety winter wood' and add ... 'I nearly wrote mood'. At other times you parody yourself, or at least your young self, in the witty sequence 'Portrait of the Poet as a Young Dog'. Do you think the raw 'I' has the right to be in a poem and that anything, no matter how personal, deeply lived transcends the personal to become universal?

A. McN: The raw 'I' has every right it can muster and I would love to hear it speak its name on the page. Or I think I would but perhaps I prefer the 'cooked' version. You have to cook the books. Really the question was settled by Rimbaud. 'I' is the ventriloquist's dummy par excellence. It belongs in the no-place of art. Once you admit that, it's all in the 'I' of the beholden. I mean the reader's eye, and in time you can be the reader of your own things just as well as anyone. I so rarely read my efforts that when I do they seem not just unsatisfactory but by someone else. The one to whom one is also beholden. If I succeed at all in my verse in self-parody etc. I fear I do so as a ventriloquist whose lips move too much. That is to say I really don't think I have succeeded at all. The art is to practise until no one sees your lips moving. But as to what has a right to be in a poem, that's something that really interests me. It brings things round to the prose-poetry connection we've already talked about, that is, the matter of mixed genres and mixed modes. Everything and anything has a right to be in a poem. It depends on the sophistication and mastery of the poet. The lyric is the predominate form of our fragmented times. In consequence we tend to have a very foreshortened view of the potential of the tradition. Every bone in my body responds to the lyrical, but that's something else. I respect most those modern and contemporary poets who manage the

36

longer poem, whether continuously or sequentially. At the same time I seem to be writing shorter and shorter poems myself. But then one has no room to negotiate. One does what comes one's way. It's involuntary more than otherwise. It's a kind of addiction too, all but impossible to give up. But it will give you up. Hence a lot of Parnassian, especially in the middle passage. Louis MacNeice is a fine example here. There are many others who go on and we indulge them, out of gratitude for their heyday. Who can blame us or them when we think how MacNeice exited, high on that burning perch?

P. McC: This playing with the 'I' seems to reach a climax in your latest collection *In Mortal Memory* where, as in John Berryman, it is never clear whether the 'I' is you or a persona. Similarly enigmatic is the addressed 'you' whose identity the reader can construct for him/herself in a multiplicity of forms. Is this a deliberate shrinking back or evolving from the raw 'I' and a kind of a mask being pulled over it?

A. McN: Well, as with the Aran book, *In Mortal Memory* is a book I continue to respect. It does play games with 'I' and 'you' and while those games are in part driven by wintry recognitions of invisibility and growing old that have real histories in the world, they are also 'no-place' games, and owe much to my reading Donne and Jonson (above all the latter's elegies), as well as to the nineteenth-century French poets. The French were wired up for me by Graham Robb's brilliant biographies which I have consumed and re-consumed with a passion. He reawakened my A-level passions for Baudelaire and the rest, the *maudits* who lived for it and died for it, very like African-American jazz musicians in the bebop era. And so the book is a step away from my 'I' as none of the previous ones have been, since the Aran memoir. It is liberating to have that kind of frame to work within. So it is both a shrinking back and an evolving. The other force here is John Berryman. Everyone has his or her 'inner-cabinet' of poets and artists, first encountered in youth and early adulthood. I read Berryman when *77 Dream Songs* first appeared on this side of the Atlantic. And I took the same kind of hit I took earlier from Dylan Thomas, both early and late Thomas. They say Thomas is the only poet to progress from adolescence to childhood. Someone has rightly called him 'durable'. He's far more than that too. But I wonder how well he's attended to for innovative courage and virtuosity and line, especially in the earlier poems? Hopkins of course is the great innovator and to my mind, Berryman. Herman Melville is also central for me. *Moby Dick* is my favourite novel and I was reading it when living on Inis Mór, as I am reading it currently. These writers pitch across the registers in ways that are startling. Donne does the same. For me Donne and Hopkins are two great poets of the twentieth century. But you can meet this rubato poetic other than in writing. After all it's a musical term. Even at the same time as I first encountered Dylan Thomas I was discovering the piano-playing and composition of Thelonious Monk, in my teenage years, in North Wales. Between us we brought North Wales and North Carolina together, little did either of us know: two non-conformist chapel traditions. The first track by Monk I ever heard was unaccompanied 'Just a Gigolo'. It took the feet out from under me. I can't quite explain why. Or couldn't then. But now I realise that Hopkins played Monkish stride piano too. His sprung rhythm was just that, it played *rubato*, just as Monk does. If you watch footage of Monk playing you see his right foot 'outriding' to the rhythm as it bodies forth through him. As if to help me make my point, Monk has a classic 'song', as he would have termed it, called 'Epistrophy' after the Greek 'epistrophe'. Originally he called it 'Pentameter'. But Monk's rhythms bend the pentameter, disrupt time and pitch up and down in the 'no-place' of art, so that tradition and the individual talent combine to 'make it new'. He played *rubato* and it was a deliberate matter. Monk was no *naïf*. No more than was Hopkins. 'This sonnet,' Hopkins wrote to Bridges about 'Spelt from Sibyl's Leaves', 'shd. be almost sung: it is most carefully timed in *tempo rubato*.' Musicologists tell you that's a difficult term to define, but that, whatever else, it refers to elasticity in tempo and rhythm, a deviation from strict clockwork. This idea has always appealed to me. There's another version of it by Sydney Graham. (Perhaps at bottom I associate strict clockwork with being employed at another's bidding.) I have sometimes written passages intended to be prose in blank verse and then broken them out, extended them, so that the prose retains the ghost of the verse, not the full accented body of it such as you get in much of Edward Thomas's prose, but just the memory of it, faintly.

P. McC: In my review of this latest book of yours, *In Mortal Memory*, in the recent *Warwick Review*, I deem you, with your blending of 'land-words' and 'sea-words', a 'master of your own tongue, a juggler with words'. This is demonstrated throughout your oeuvre. As a proper craftsman, including an accomplished sonneteer, and a free verse exponent, what is your attitude to formality in poetry today?

A. McN: I am a formalist, it seems. Nor am I persuaded that Yeats hammered the last nail into the coffin of rhetoric when he proclaimed that 'The rhetorician would deceive his neighbour / ... While art is but a vision of reality'. After all, some today would dismiss Yeats as a rhetorician merely. I admire and envy the early modern poets for their rhetorical skills and their powers of ventriloquy and their formalities. To write a poem that others might consider to be a poem and even to be good is not the best one can hope for. The best is to believe in one's endeavour, regardless. There is always, and will ever be, a disproportionately great quantity of bad verse, free or otherwise. I really don't care what other people get up to or how if it doesn't knock me off my feet at once. It's their business not mine.

P. McC: What other poets in the past have influenced you and who do you most admire today?

A. McN: Well, I think I have largely answered this, in speaking of Donne and Jonson (my two favourite contemporaries) and Hopkins. But I have to add Wordsworth (up to 1805) and Edward Thomas, Eliot and Pound, MacDiarmid, Sorley MacLean, George Campbell Hay, Iain Crichton Smith, Edwin Morgan, Ivor Gurney, David Jones, John Berryman, Dylan Thomas. As to those alive today, I am not going to begin to say. Through the Clutag Press and my magazine *Archipelago*, I've had the privilege of publishing many of the significant British and Irish poets writing in the past thirty years. As a publisher one must be catholic, to an extent, but I have never published work I don't love or greatly admire.

P. McC: How important do you consider it is to develop as a poet, in subject matter and in technique?

A. McN: As much as I consider it important to develop as a person. That's the starting place. But one is always tethered historically, rooted somewhere and in some cultural nexus, resist it as one might. I mean my moorings are somewhere in the 1960s, probably, if not earlier. Technical innovation is a form of resistance, resistance to a norm or norms, but the very nature of being in a state of resistance is inflected by what one is resisting. If one finds a 'new' subject or 'new subject matter' then it should follow that technique goes in hand with the discovery, and shifts the ground. But some poets write more or less the same poem over and over and do that so well it doesn't matter that there's no technical development to speak of. Think of Housman, for example. (Though Housman's oeuvre is far more diverse than the *Shropshire Lad* poems suggest.)

P. McC: I notice you always have a sense of play, of playing with words, with quotations, with the juxtaposition of humour and seriousness ('deeply gravity may depend on laughter'), how you refresh our common parlance, particularly in *In Mortal Memory*, by playing with and inverting hollow clichés, and by playing with the identity of the 'I' in a poem. Is this derived, deep down, from Beckett and existentialism, and from the suspicion that nothing lasts except the word?

A. McN: I think some people find this 'play' irritating but I can't help myself. I believe in it too, innately. It is maybe a 'Celtic' thing, and I do believe it derives from my upbringing in Wales quite as much as my preference for certain Irish writers. Is it in Ireland an expression of colonial exclusion, a last resort from a world in which one has no other voice but to amuse oneself with words as objects, as things, as a game with which to pass the hour or indeed to kill time? Although I had a phase when I doted on Beckett, especially the novel *Watt*, I don't think I can explain myself in terms of his thought. I hope I do celebrate the world and rejoice in it quite as much as I play upon the strings of sorrow. The play with clichés is early modern. I haven't yet mentioned Andrew Marvell, but I am fascinated by his manipulation of cliché and often sit staring at, for example, the opening stanzas to 'Upon Appleton House' to try to fathom what's going on there. Berryman is the other figure in the frame for me here, and of course he couldn't have written as he did without the early modern writers.

P. McC: I love what you say about the word: that you 'put your faith' in it: 'The word made gooseflesh, tingling with remembrance, joy and sorrow, the soul made flesh, grounded in the world'. Here you have, on the other hand, it seems, a kind of pagan religiosity, veering towards mysticism. Whoever dares use the word 'soul' these days – sadly? Can you comment on this?

A. McN: Well, I do dare. I do also dare to speak of 'truth' and 'faith' and also to blaspheme and to praise the Word. And I hope some trace of what those terms have meant, survives in my adulterated usage. Poetry is my religion. I begin most days by reading a poem or two, taken at random from my 'inner cabinet' or from an anthology. I always did so when at OUP, just to help survive the madness of office life. Ideally one should have a place, time, and space in which to read aloud.

P. McC: Place is obviously important to you. Indeed, it seems that in you all the maps, coastlines, latitudes and longitudes of Wales, Scotland, England and Ireland, including all the surging lines of the Irish Sea, merge. Does this give you a feeling of belonging, or, paradoxically, of not belonging except to that 'native self' who is perhaps ultimately placeless and belongs nowhere?

A. McN: The will to belong is surely heightened in these nomadic 'global' times. I recognize when I go to my native country that everything about it seems to fit me like a glove, everything but community, because I am too long absent. A place is important if one was imprinted on it and a certain aesthetics will take hold, informed by all manner of things, from Dylan

Thomas's estuarine poetry, from Wordsworth's 'Prelude', the land and seascapes of Kyffin Williams... I grew up never more than a quarter of a mile from the Irish Sea, and for the period of my adolescent awakening, within sight of it, within sight of northern Snowdonia, Penmaenmawr, Ynys Môn, Ynys Seiriol, the Great Orme, the Conwy estuary. For me these things were as foundational as my father's voice. It's not a matter of putting them in your kitbag, they are the kitbag, they are a moveable feast and serve you powerfully when you are away from their origin, or when you visit places in which similar qualities are found. I have said I don't belong anywhere. But I would correct that now. I have belongings in a number of places, but the two most potent are not places I come from directly: they are the Machars of Wigtownshire and Inis Mór, and that's not a matter of physical features and aesthetics but of community, of people.

P. McC: The past is also important to you, usually along with the place. In *Slower,* for example, you fuse beautifully Welsh history and myth with the politics of our present day, along with your own personal mythology. What different reasons have you for doing this?

A. McN: 'Reason' is a strong term. I'm not sure I reasoned it so much as felt it as I went along. I assume you are referring to the Glyn Dŵr poems. (I do still respect those, too.) I'd earmarked Glyn Dŵr as a subject I wanted to write a poem about years before, but could get nothing off the ground. Then Osama Bin Laden blasted his way to prominence with a surprise attack very like Owain Glyn Dŵr's in 1400. That was the donnée. I was also hooked on the challenge of the sonnet, and wanting to do it *rubato*, to have the liberating benefit of the tight form, while bending the measure, leaving enjambements hanging in mid-air, playing with all manner of rhymes, direct, half-, internal in the Welsh style, and eye-rhymes. It all started to happen, everything singing and dancing together, and I wrote the twenty-eight in a fine fit of excitement and anxiety, anxiety because if I couldn't find the 'next' one, all the effort to that point would not add up to a poem. The *cynghangedd* effects and the like, internal rhyming and so on, just happened. I never worked at them. They seem to be natural to me. Of course they can only be a gesture at the Welsh practice which is elaborate and precise and powerfully enabled my mutation. *Cynghangedd* means harmony. Things are gained in 'translation' as well as lost, and for me the gain is in the direction of disharmony and noise. It's word play, of course, and there's a new breed of reader and critic who has no time for it. I once addressed a poem to one who said in a review: 'Our age prefers a light touch' ..., to which I added: 'Someone's acquired a plural, / someone's acquired an age. / If it isn't too much trouble / may time prove his scourge.'

As to working my own personal mythology in, it seemed only right to ironise my intervention, both as to addressing the 'Great Game' as it was kicking off again in Afghanistan, and as to being as I am Welsh only by dint of being born there (and spending the first twenty years of my life there, barring six months or so). Wales has been very generous to me, but far from all Welsh people would allow me to be Welsh. I can't speak Welsh beyond a few preliminaries, though I was taught it compulsorily to the age of fourteen, and sometimes I realise I know more Welsh than I think I do. If I lived there I would get up to colloquial speed quite quickly.

P. McC: Do you think politics should be confronted head-on in poetry, or rather, as Seamus Heaney suggests, taken only at an angle in order to avoid the poem becoming a political slogan?

A. McN: Well, Seamus Heaney is well-known to be expert in analogy. Whether more direct approaches necessarily result in mere 'sloganising' I am not sure. Of course they might well. I'm thinking of Marvell, master of the even-hand and the oblique. But there are some far more direct political poems in his oeuvre, in Latin, for example, as there are in Milton, and they are powerful; and I think Alistair Macdonald wrote devastatingly direct political poems in the flyting style, and Burns did some pretty direct stuff that rises above sloganising and MacDiarmid also, and Yeats. The tradition is different in Scotland. Part of the problem in the English language tradition as we have it now, is that it is essentially given over to the lyric. Other modes – satirical not least – hardly find expression. Geoffrey Hill is much driven by this difficulty and has I think mastered it, exquisitely. But 'head-on' is a blunt instrument and effectively fulfils your point and guarantees agreement.

P. McC: Much of the strength of your poetry lies in the way you are not afraid to deal with love and loss. Like a Romantic poet, you say somewhere, 'But once we've dreamt it, how we can't/ help but mourn it', and, more tellingly perhaps, 'the path to truth begins in loss'. Your poetry is full of laments, homages and haunting elegies, full of the loss of love, the loved one forever elusive and elsewhere. You say, in the final finely-wrought sonnet from the sequence 'Arkwork' about the sinking of the Princess Victoria in 1953, that you would 'go down again with the good ship Elegy/ on a dog-toothed covenant wing-and-prayer/ to see all the world as it flashed before me.' Is the elegy, then, the best resting place and springboard of the poem?

A. McN: Goodness, I never forget Peter McDonald telling me that 'elegy is the album verse of our time'. And as you know I've written a couple of little poems seeking (in vain) to lay it to rest. Who would like to think they write album-verse? I hope my poems are too angular and awkward for that. But I am a melancholic on the downside of my joy in 'mortal beauty' – 'To what serves mortal beauty – dangerous' says Hopkins, catching at the heart of the problem. The poems about the Princess Victoria came from a family connection. My wife is distantly related to David Broadfoot, the radio operator who as he went down repeatedly signalled for help heroically to his last breath. Hearing of this made me think about the business of the verse elegy, the great examples, to tragedies at sea, and the work they do, as works of art, to memorialise – as Milton does in 'Lycidas' and Hopkins in 'The Wreck of the Deutschland', both of which are also very much about far more than their ostensible subjects. Otherwise as to elegy and loss, surely it is true in that we live in a fallen world, and are compulsive recidivists, and that 'the path to truth begins in loss'?

P. McC: I like your fusing of the lyric with the discursive, avoiding all didacticism in both your poetry and your prose. Is this important in poetry today, do you think?

A. McN: I don't know that I know enough about 'poetry today' to say. This fusion business is none the less a driving thing for me. I do hope I avoid didacticism though, and it encourages me that you say I do.

P. McC: In *Slower*, for example, you criticise subtly any poetry collection that is a mere 'box of vanities' – 'the place most poems meet their end.' Conversely, at the end of 'Homage to Patagonia', you tender knowingly: 'The poem can wait until it can't wait'. If a poem has to be essential, forced out of the poet, with that mysterious engine behind it, how far, then, do you think that a poet can be 'made' by writing more-or-less to order (for example in Creative Writing departments of universities), rather than be 'born'?

A. McN: I was referring to the 'box of vanities' that was my juvenilia, but of course boxes of vanities are published all the time. It's not for me to worry about that. If I don't like a book or a poem I generally keep that to myself. No one else needs to know. I don't attempt to review poetry any more. Though I am deeply indebted to you for undertaking to review me, I think reviewing's too often a footling exercise and besides I am always too soft on the offender – so I'm just not able for it. I'm afraid I do believe that the craft of poetry can and must be learnt, by personal trial and error, but it can't be taught. I believe you must be 'maimed for it', in Sydney Graham's phrase. I think 'creative writing' is an offensive idea. It implies something precious, and is a direct cousin to the world of the managerial career-monkeys, who want everything homogenised. Otherwise the whole human endeavour is creative. We don't speak of 'creative' musical composition, or 'creative' engineering, or 'creative' scholarship or 'creative' parenting (I hope). As Charlie Parker said, on the question of jazz and other forms, 'it's all just music'. Latterly I have been running an MA at the University of Exeter's campus in Cornwall, called 'Writing, Nature and Place', and essential to it is teaching ways of writing non-fictional prose. So I'm especially sensitive to the issue, and uneasy. And I think of my father turning in his grave.

P. McC: Is this too ideal a view of mine that few have the right to write unless, single-mindedly like you, they can say, 'I have lived for language, and the word, to my cost now, as well as to my gain... following my muse'.

A. McN: Everyone has the right to write, surely, but not to expect publication. I wish everyone would write the story of his or her life, a view I share with Leslie Stephen, Virginia Woolf's father, and the original editor of the *Dictionary of National Biography*. Woolf herself – as might surprise some to know – very much shared this democratic view. There's a lot of 'self-publishing' goes on now, through the web, and who knows what posterity will make of it. But if someone else will publish you, that's special, even today when far too many books are published. You need that but you need also to go on whether you're published or not. The delayed event that was my book about Aran, is a case in point. You have to need to go on. If you don't need to, then you escape scot-free and are very lucky indeed.

P. McC: Your wonderful book, *An Aran Keening,* should be on the shelf of every 'word shod' person in the universe, along with your poetry, which it also is. Therein snorts 'the Grey Fella', a kind of Pegasus – 'the finest, flintiest, limestone-enriched, charcoal-dappled animal you ever met on the road, coming at a trot on the halter, showing his paces at Galway Fair'. And we'll leave him there, half-broken in, nostrils flaring at the edge of the world, against 'the back-roar of the sea'.

Rachel Faulkner

Rachel Faulkner is 23 and grew up in Dorset. She studied English Literature at Cardiff University and is now completing a Master's degree at the University of Warwick.

The Farrier

The farrier worked his knife
between the frog and where the hoof grows hard
and like a fingernail.

Damp head pressed with trust
against the great bay's belly,
he dug the abscess out, with a grunt and hiss
like the freeing of a cork.

After he had left
I washed the empty yard clean with water.
Tossing full buckets on the red stains.
It made the colours in the blood
fan out, like an oil slick.
And the smell, vinegar and bile.

So all the while I had to think of his great face.
Sleepy black eyes, and breath,
warm still but slower. Seeking out
the rest of my lowered shoulder.

Colic

Though his eyes, shining black buttons,
plunge into mine, sleep gathering
in their corners, beads of sweat blinking
on his long lashes like precious stones.

Though his body shivers in the heat,
and his shoulders lean with forceful trust
against my hip, his hind leg kicking up
at his belly as if to smash a fly.

We must not let him down,
each crack of the stick against his flank
rings into the darkness like gunfire.

Gavin Goodwin

Gavin Goodwin was born in 1977 and grew up in Newport, South Wales. He studied English and Creative Writing at Cardiff University. Gavin's poems have appeared in *Fire* magazine, and the 2008 Cinnamon Press anthology, *Black Waves in Cardiff Bay*.

Winter Horses

Almost blind, she walks from the estate
down thin lanes to the farm. Knapsack
stretched over her winter coat, grey hair
tied in a ponytail, under a green cap.

A blackbird hops from the hedgerow,
a brown bull snorts: steam leaking
from wet nostrils. She hears an engine,
leans in to the bushes.
A Ford Fiesta thumps by.

At the farm she opens the iced door
of the caravan. Prongs of blue flame
splash the base of the kettle. She unlocks
the wooden stable – warmth of horses,
damp hay underfoot, their breath wets her face.

*

She fends off pneumonia, but returns
from hospital with the last of her sight
dissolved in darkness. Forced to give up
the lease on the farm, she sits, now,
confined to her box flat, listening
to television, or noise
of neighbours throbbing through the ceiling.

On a quiet morning she remembers
raising her small white hand, horse dipping
his long face. The dark globes of his eyes
softening – she imagines them softening –
feeling him nuzzle into her cold palm,
hearing his tail brush the stable wall.

Josephine Balmer

It Happens Once For Ever

Seamus Heaney: *Human Chain*, Faber, 2010
Robert Henryson: *The Testament of Cresseid & Seven Fables*: translated by
Seamus Heaney, Faber, 2009
Derek Mahon: *An Autumn Wind*, The Gallery Press, 2010
Derek Walcott: *White Egrets*, Faber, 2010
Aidan Andrew Dun: *McCool*, Goldmark, 2010

Sometimes, as translation scholar Susan Bassnett recently observed, a writer
wants to write something that has already been written. 'And the only way
to do that,' she notes, 'is to write it again.' If, like the poets reviewed here,
there is an accumulation of literary and lifetime experience on which to draw
(Derek Walcott is 80 this year, Seamus Heaney and Derek Mahon both in
their seventh decades), then the need for rewriting becomes more acute. As
Heaney's new collection *Human Chain* confirms – the first since he suffered
a major stroke in 2006 – it is often only by looking back that a writer can also
look forward. In addition, there is an almost ominous sense of time passing,
the metaphoric emptying of grain from a bag, as its title poem concludes:

> A letting go which will not come again,
> Or it will, once. And for all.

Throughout his previous collections, Heaney's 'letting go' has seen him
return over and over again to the past, from the idyllic landscapes of a rural
Derry childhood on his parents' farm to the scarring violence of political
and religious divides in the north of Ireland, which have become recurrent
themes in his poetry, a means of rewriting his own verse. *Human Chain* is
no exception; alongside the 'special militiamen' of 'The Wood Road' and
the revival of his 1983 mythological protagonist in 'Sweeny Out-Takes,' the
poems are dotted with apron bibs, ashplants, enamel pails and scullions, even,
in 'An Old Refrain', '*a hey-nonny-no*'. As 'A Herbal' asks of lost childhood
games in graveyard meadows:

> Where can it be found again,
> An elsewhere world, beyond
>
> Maps and atlases,
> Where all is woven into

And of itself, like a nest
Of crosshatched grass blades?

Yet Heaney's art transcends nostalgia. From the single translations that have graced his collections since 1979's *Field Work* to his much-lauded *Beowulf* in 1999 and beyond, he is one of the most rigorous and successful rewriters of ancient texts in contemporary English. Similarly *Human Chain* includes versions of Latin epic, early Irish lyrics, as well as of the more modern European verse of Guillevic and Giovanni Pascoli. Such work moves the poet forward, the means by which he can approach the trauma of his stroke in the tender 'Chanson d'Aventure' (its title a nod to early medieval genre), and, like Orpheus, enter the realm of the dead unscathed. In particular, his masterly versions of Aeneas's trip to the Underworld in Virgil's *Aeneid* VI, 'The Riverbank Field' and the 12-poem sequence 'Route 110', form the still-beating heart of the collection. Here Virgil's gloomy geography of Hades is transformed, as ever, into Heaney's childhood Derry with typical precision, inventiveness and wit; the crowded ghosts of Charon's barge, which Virgil likened to falling autumn leaves, become a tightly-packed rack of market stall coats. Similarly, lost souls waiting to be directed to their otherworldly destinations are bus station passengers called out by an inspector to their respective routes.

Heaney emerges refreshed from Hades; 'Route 110' ends not with a death but a birth, that of his first granddaughter, to whom the sequence is dedicated. And the collection concludes on a note of elation: even as the poet of 'In the Attic' ages, blanking on names or uncertain on stairs, he comes full circle to an ever-present, ever-parallel childhood world of *Treasure Island*, recovering the thrill of a cabin boy's first time on the riggings:

It's not that I can't imagine still
That slight untoward rapture and world-tilt
As a wind freshened and anchor weighed.

In his introduction to his new version of the medieval Scots poet Robert Henryson, *The Testament of Cresseid & Seven Fables,* Heaney acknowledges this therapeutic power of rewriting foundation texts, citing Eliot Weinberger's motive of 'writing by proxy' as one of the main impetus for undertaking such projects; re-reading Henryson, he notes, he experienced the same 'transfusion' Dryden had found through working on Chaucer. Nevertheless Henryson's often dour and, to modern sensibilities, morally ambiguous fables, themselves based on Aesop's Greek originals, might at first seem an odd coupling for Heaney. But reading the contemporary poet's appreciation of his medieval forebear, a writer, he notes, only too able to handle an 'easy passage between the oral and learned culture... an intelligence stretched between the homely and the homiletic', one can appreciate the suitability of the match. Heaney's version ably captures both the metaphysical and earthy qualities of Henryson's Scots, helping us to appreciate, unlike the eponymous cock in 'The Cock and the Jasper,' the worth of a gemstone hidden under dust and ashes:

> First, as to colour, it is marvellous,
> Like fire, partly, partly like the heaven.
> It makes a man strong and victorious,
> Preserves him too when things turn dangerous.

As well as the intellectual rewards of working with Henryson, Heaney also explains that he was drawn by a more physical pull; an early medieval manuscript of the Scots poems which he came across at a British Library exhibition.

In *An Autumn Wind* Heaney's friend and slightly younger contemporary Derek Mahon is also inspired by the industry of medieval monasticism, the monks of the tiny island of Sceilig Mhichíl in western Ireland:

> whose dim lights glimmered in a distant age
> to illuminate at the edge
> a future life.

('At the Butler Arms')

For Mahon, such endeavours are the remnants of a greater, golden age, safe from 'the dense refrain/of wailing siren, truck and train/and incoherent cries' of the contemporary world as 'The Thunder Shower' explains. Like Heaney, too, Mahon is an experienced translator, who finds inspiration – and comfort – in the rewriting of older texts. *An Autumn Wind* offers reworkings of Homer's *Odyssey*, Baudelaire (recontextualised, as its title reveals, to Belfast's 'Antrim Road'), Rimbaud and Quevedo while Mahon evokes Pound in his versions of classical Chinese lyric and echoes Peter Russell's pseudo *The Elegies of Quintilius* in his own psuedo-translations of the fictitious Hindi poet Gopal Singh. As in Heaney's *Human Chain*, many of the collection's poems find sanctuary in the pastoral of rural Ireland, particularly Mahon's west Cork home, where, with 'no Google goggling at our marginal lives,' as 'The Seasons' notes, 'there are still corners where a lark can sing.' Certainly Mahon's verse seems most satisfying when present pessimism gives way to future hope, its success often in inverse proportion to its sense of dislocation.

As 'An Aspiring Spirit', his assured and affecting version of Quevedo's sonnet, ends:

> There will be ashes, yes, but smouldering ashes;
> there will be dust, but dust glowing with love.

Derek Walcott is also renowned for his inventive and innovative rewriting of foundation texts, most notably *Omeros,* his epic 1990 version of Homer's *Odyssey,* which contributed to his award of the Nobel Prize in 1992. Yet while his technical virtuosity has often been highly praised, his collections have been criticised for their lack of focus; as William Logan commented 'what you remember... is the texture, never the text'. Such judgements fail to appreciate the underlying classicism of Walcott's work in which single units of poems work towards a collective whole, inextricably linked. *White Egrets* is no exception, its breathless enjambements, highly skilled use of rhyme and interlocking imagery – of sea, land and sky, alongside the ever-present egrets themselves – draw the reader on through 54 poems and 89 pages like the 'ceaselessly charging whitecaps ' of Walcott's Caribbean waves until, in poem 54:

> a cloud slowly covers the page and it goes
> white again and the book comes to a close.

Walcott's poetic sensibility is so attuned it can distinguish, in 'Sicilian Suite', between the heat of Italy and that of his home on St Lucia ('the way the oleanders looked and the olive's green flame'). Yet, as it should be, it is also hard to pin down, vanishing through the hands like mist. Above all he is a poet of water and air, the most difficult elements to capture in any medium. As in a Turner painting, steam rises from the collection's pages like a sea-fret, that candescent horizon where:

> Light hurls its nets
> over the whitecaps and seagulls grieve
> over some common but irreplaceable loss

> (poem 30)

With Heaney and Mahon, Walcott, too, is haunted by such losses: of friends, of colleagues, of health, of youth, of love, whether the newer, unrequited affair of 'Sicilian Suite' or an old flame chanced upon again 'her devastating/ smile was netted in wrinkles' in 'Sixty Years After'. Nevertheless, the collection's many settings from Syracuse to Barcelona, Amsterdam, London and New York, as well as Walcott's home on St Lucia, reflect the exhausting itineraries of today's international super-poet, which would defeat many younger men. For Walcott, far from looking backwards towards a golden age of childhood, the present and the past merge into one as, in poem 30, he surveys 'a sea so / deep it has lost its stuttering memory of our hates'. Even the imperialist ghosts which stalk the 'The Lost Empire', their victories now 'air', their 'dominions dirt', are as nothing to 'the wild light that loosens/a galloping mare on the plain of Vieuxfort'. This is the poetry of possibility, of hope, in which, as Walcott attests in poem 51, there is 'so much to do still, all of it praise'. Here the Old World and its culture – Petrarch, Wyatt and Surrey, El Greco, Canaletto – are filtered through the brilliant light, the white heat, turquoise sea and bird cry of the New. As Walcott counsels himself in poem 32:

> be grateful that you wrote well in this place,
> let the torn poems sail from you like a flock
> of white egrets in a long last sigh of release.

A former protégé of Walcott, Aidan Andrew Dun is younger than the other poets reviewed here and far less known. Published in beautiful editions by Goldmark, a branch of the art gallery which also first discovered the equally numinous prose of Iain Sinclair, Dun operates almost completely outside the orthodoxies of the poetry world. Yet his poetic concerns are similar to his mentors; *Vale Royal*, Dun's first long narrative work, unearthed a mystical Arthurian quest in north London, presenting an unlikely but nevertheless compelling spiritual journey through the literary and mythological landscapes of King's Cross. His latest work, the verse novel *McCool*, transposes Homeric epic, Gilgamesh, and Irish myth to a near-future world of constant warfare in the Middle East, employing, like Vikram Seth before him, Pushkin's challenging sonnet form from *Eugene Onegin*. As in *Vale Royal*, Dun's technical virtuosity and compelling sense of place underline a unique poetic vision, well worth exploring:

> June in the vast metropolis.
> The city like a sinking ship
> dives in a flame through an abyss
> of houses, towers; seems to slip
> down an incline of despair,
> through a filthy atmosphere
> of getting as opposed to giving...

Dun is another poet concerned with the loss that comes with experience, of a world once known, a loss of innocence. Their joint comfort for such loss is a strong sense of place, a sheltering ground, whether Derry, Cork, St Lucia or London. But for poets, sanctuary can be found not just in a place to enter but in a text to inhabit. And if their work is haunted by the knowledge that civilisations might fall and their literature become redundant, they understand, too, as all these collections prove so conclusively, that from the rubble of the old, new – and equal – texts emerge, the latter energising and refreshing the former. As Derek Mahon confirms in 'A Country Kitchen', dedicated to Seamus Heaney:

if a thing happens once
it happens once for ever.

David Cooke

The City is a Map of the City

Ciaran Carson: *Collected Poems*, Gallery Press, 2008. Paperback.

Although poetry and politics have been inextricably entwined in Northern Ireland, the poets have often been guarded in the face of expectations that they should in some way be self-consciously 'responding' to a political situation. Seamus Heaney famously entitled a poem 'Whatever You Say Say Nothing' in response to 'an English journalist in search of "views" / on the Irish thing.' However, of all the major voices to have emerged from the province, Ciaran Carson, recently dubbed 'Belfast's unofficial poet laureate' by Hugh McFadden, is the one whose work has been most directly affected by the day to day experience of living with sectarian violence and military occupation. Published in 2008 to coincide with his sixtieth birthday, Carson's *Collected Poems* includes virtually the entire contents of his eight previous collections. Born in 1948 into an Irish speaking Catholic family in Belfast, Carson has spent all his life in the city, a fact which distinguishes his work from that of his fellow Catholics, Heaney or Muldoon, who both grew up in rural communities.

The New Estate, Carson's first collection published in 1976, was a wonderfully achieved debut that showed that what he had in common with his elders, Heaney, Longley and Mahon, was his concern for craftsmanship, clarity, and cadence. As might be expected, there are in fact occasional echoes of their work. 'Linen' for example is reminiscent of Longley:

> From the photographs of bleach greens
> Mill-hands stare across the snowy acres.
> In a frieze white as marble
> Their lives are ravelled and unravelled –

In 'King's Lynn' one can also detect the influence of Heaney: 'Estuaries silt up, / Lost in a choke of mud. / Fields mutate / to another branch of the sea.' Nevertheless, Carson had already developed his own voice and a distinctive range of interests. As a native speaker of Irish it is not surprising to find poems based on early Irish mythology such as 'The Insular Celts' or 'St Ciaran's Island'. There are also versions of early Irish or Welsh poetry. An accomplished musician himself, his fine ear for phrasing comes through in the opening lines of 'O'Carolan's Complaint':

The great tunes
I never played are lost
To monied patronage, the lit rooms
In grey façades

Whisper, fall silent
At their harmony and grace. I think
Of all the girls I might have loved
Instead of music –

However, where Carson is at his most affecting is in those poems which deal with family life and the quiet pleasures of domesticity. In 'An Early Bed' he finds himself redecorating the bedroom in which he used to sleep as a child and is reminded by an earlier layer of wallpaper of how he was once punished for raising his hand against his father: 'A child who struck his father, / He once told me, died / Soon afterwards.' In 'Twine' he describes the inside of his father's postman's sack: 'I stuck my head inside / The canvas flap and breathed the gloom. // The smell of raffia and faded ink / Was like the smell of nothing.' Carson's ability to re-create the physical actuality of an object is something he shares with Heaney and has remained one of his trademarks. In 'To a Married Sister' patches of damp have 'the sluggish tints of an old map'. Emptying boxes, he notices 'the hairline net / Of cracks on worn enamel' and notes how 'A gold resin / Leaked from the slackened joints' of cheap furniture. The precision and detail of these poems is such that one might imagine the poet were living in a world as self-contained and calm as that of Vermeer. It is only in 'Bomb Disposal' that we get any sense of the violence on the streets outside and an indication of the direction Carson's work will take:

Is it just like picking a lock
With the slow deliberation of a funeral,
Hesitating through a darkened nave
Until you find the answer? [...]

The city is a map of the city,
Its forbidden areas changing daily.
I find myself in a crowded taxi
Making deviations from the known route,

The New Estate gave every indication that Carson was one to watch. However, apart from *The Lost Explorer,* a modest pamphlet published by

The Honest Ulsterman in 1978, a decade would pass before he brought out another collection.

The silence was eventually broken in 1987 by the publication of *The Irish for No* which was followed in 1990 by *Belfast Confetti*. Both collections were radically different from his earlier work and are breathtaking not only in their imaginative sweep but also in the brilliance of their technique. Abandoning his traditional stanzas, Carson now favoured a much longer line which seemed to have something in common with the work of the American poet C.K. Williams. He may also have been influenced by some of the longer, loping lines of Irish ballads and the tradition of Gaelic singing known as *sean-nós* ('the old-style'). In both collections the new line is put to two different uses. The poems are either long freewheeling narratives or shorter more focused pieces of nine lines grouped into two stanzas of five and four respectively. The latter have the appearance of block-built sonnets and seem particularly appropriate to Carson's urban terrain.

'Dresden', the opening poem of the *Irish for No,* is five pages long and is apparently about a man called Horse Boyle who joined the RAF in the Second World War, and who took part in the bombing of Dresden. However, one is a long way into the poem before such facts emerge:

> Horse Boyle was called Horse Boyle because of his brother Mule;
> Though why Mule was called Mule is anybody's guess. I stayed there once,
> Or rather, I nearly stayed there once. But that's another story...

The narrator then goes on to describe 'the decrepit caravan' where Boyle lived 'Encroached upon by baroque pyramids of empty baked bean tins...' However, as one thing leads to another he reminisces about old fashioned shop bells, the smells of tobacco, Ulster fries, and a mortar bomb attack which then reminds him of another character called Flynn. Over the course of a few lines we learn how this new individual got locked up by accident, but learned 'The best of Irish' in jail and how 'He had thirteen words for a cow in heat'. Jam packed with etymology, history and proverbial wisdom, the poem is also replete with grim humour and pathos. Eventually we learn that Horse Boyle was a rear gunner and that 'Of all the missions, Dresden broke his heart. It reminded him of china' and 'in particular a figure from his childhood, a milkmaid / Standing on the mantelpiece.' It is clear that what is important here is not so much the tale as the way of telling it. A traditional storyteller like a musician must, to use the Gaelic term, have his own *blas,* his own unique accent or flavour.

In the shorter poems Carson charts in minute detail the sights, sounds and topography of his city's divided streets. In 'Belfast Confetti' we see the riot squad moving in with their 'Makrolon face-shields' and 'Walkie-talkies' under the hail of missiles which give the poem its title. We are also shown in 'Bloody Hand' how matter-of-fact attitudes to violence can become:

> *Your man*, says the Man, *will walk into the bar like this* – here his fingers
> Mimic a pair of legs, one stiff at the knee – *so you'll know exactly*
> *What to do*. He sticks his finger to his head.

In these poems and in the prose pieces that accompany them in *Belfast Confetti* Carson's project is not unlike that of the exiled James Joyce who also tried to evoke in encyclopaedic detail his own Dublin streets. In 'The Exiles' Club' Carson even describes a group of Belfast ex-pats in Australia who meet up for the same purpose: 'After years they have reconstructed the whole of the Falls Road, and now / Are working on the backstreets: Lemon, Peel and Omar, Balaklava, Alma. // They just about keep up with the news of bombings and demolition…'

The Irish for No and *Belfast Confetti* are Carson's analogue of Joyce's *Ulysses*. With his 1993 collection *First Language* his work undergoes a further sea change and takes him closer to the Joyce of *Finnegans Wake,* as language itself becomes a theme for much of the work. Carson's 'first language' is of course Irish and in his dedicatory poem to his wife in that language, he speaks directly of his own feelings in a way that he does not in English:

> Your mouth pressed unexpectedly
> Upon my mouth
> And I was absorbed completely
> In the deep twilight of your kiss.

> (My translation)

Yet when it comes to the poet's 'second language' he lets the auditory imagination run wild:

> English not being yet a language, I wrapped my lubber lips
>   around my thumb.
> Brain-deaf as an embryo, I was snuggled in my comfort-
>   blanket dumb.

Growling figures campaniled above me, and twanged their
      carillons of bronze
Sienna consonants embedded with the vowels *alexandrite,*
      emerald and *topaz.*

From the poem's echoes of Rimbaud's sonnet 'Voyelles' it is clear that new influences are at play and elsewhere in the collection he includes a reworking of Baudelaire's 'Correspondances', another of the sacred texts of the French Symbolists, and after them the Surrealists, influences which go some way in explaining the outrageous risks Carson is now taking with language. However, in a recent interview in the *Guardian* he gives a further clue as to what he may be trying to achieve, when he refers to one of his earliest memories of drifting off to sleep as a child and listening to the sound of horses in the street: 'I would think 'horse' and the Irish *'capall'*. And the sound of *'capall'* to me was 'horse', whereas 'horse' sounded exotic and odd'. Perhaps too, the Irish word more clearly evoked the clatter of a horse's hooves, sounding as it does almost the same as the English word 'cobble'. What is beyond doubt is that throughout *First Language* the poet is driven by his pure delight in sounds. Take, for example, 'Grass', another of his shaggy dog stories about some characters who may be paramilitaries and who have just 'done a deal of blow':

      ...when in the general boggledybotch, the budgie
Unlatched himself from out the room, and what cheeped and
Canterburied
Wasn't Gospel – which hardly gave a fiddler's, since the flats were on
the bias
Or on the juice.

It was the circumbendibus of everything that got us locked
And scuttered, the Anno Domini of what had happened yonks before
Our time and that is why we languish now in Anguagela Jail, while he
Is on the loose.

In *Bagpipe Music* language is not only stripped of meaning but even assumes the rhythm of a jig: 'He came lilting down the brae with a blackthorn stick the thick of a shotgun / In his fist, going, *blah dithery dump a doodle scattery idle fortunoodle.*' It is also no coincidence that this is the first of Carson's collections where he uses rhyme to a significant degree. In any language the existence of rhyme is of course quite fortuitous, but this is grist to Carson's mill, as in '58' where the poem is driven along by a series of triple near rhymes:

They'd rehearsed the usual Heinz variety of condoms, clocks, fertilizer,
    and electrical flex,
Plus a Joker's device which, someone claimed had devolved
    from one of the Fifties *Batman* serial flicks –
Which proves there's nothing new *sub specie aeternitatis*,
    or it's part of the general Heraclitean flux.

Moreover, the 'rhymes' are deployed in such a way as to mimic the singsong rhythms of a grammar school kid rattling out Latin declensions: 'flex/flicks/flux', 'caff/kiff/cuff' etc, echoing the effect of 'hic/haec/hoc', or the pattern that a student hears when learning the irregular verbs in Carson's 'second language': 'sing/sang/ sung', 'drink/drank/drunk'.

In 'The Ark of the Covenant' he writes four variants of the same poem, as if he were a jazz musician using the chord changes of one melody to create a new one, which is then used as the basis for a further improvisation. This technique is used again in 'The Ballad of HMS Belfast'. Having already produced a 'version' of Rimbaud's *'Le Bateau ivre'*, Carson then writes his own poem inspired by it, in which he brings together the Irish ballad and *le Symbolisme* to create an *aisling* or dream poem:

On the first day of April, *Belfast* disengaged her moorings, and
    sailed away
From old Belfast. Sealed orders held our destination,
    somewhere in the Briny Say.

Our crew of Jacks was aromatic with tobacco-twist and
    alcoholic
Reekings from the night before. Both Cathestants and
    Protholics.

In the course of its twenty five stanzas the reader is taken on a rollicking journey through hallucinatory seascapes, that *dérèglement de tous les sens* advocated by Rimbaud, until ironically the protagonist, an archetypal Irish patriot, awakes with a bump: 'bound in iron chains... on board the prison ship *Belfast*'.

In 1996 Carson followed *First Language* with *Opera Et Cetera,* the title of which almost suggests that its contents may be slightly redundant after the copiousness and the inspired pyrotechnics of its predecessor. Indeed, Carson has hinted as much himself: 'the whole enterprise of *Opus Et Cetera* was partly willed and mechanical, partly arbitrary and given.' It's as if after the symphonic sweep of *First Language* he then decided to rework similar material in a book of études. The collection consists of three sequences. There are two based upon the letters of the alphabet in its standard form and then again in its phonetic or 'military' version. These are separated by a shorter sequence of eleven poems which are inspired by Latin tags. Apart from the opening poem, all the remaining pieces are written in five long-lined rhyming couplets. Unfortunately, a certain monotony soon sets in as the poems demonstrate the steady application of the journeyman rather than the brilliance of *le voyant*. The poem 'A' gives an indication of Carson's procedures as the shape of the letter A evokes the image of a Stealth bomber:

> Invisible to radar, *Stealth* glided through their retina of sweep
>   and dot.
> No bleep appeared to register its Alpha wing. The watchers were asleep,
>   or not.
>
> An Ampoule-bomb lay ampere wired-up in it, waiting for its
>   primal sec-
> Ond, like its embryonic A becoming Be. It wanted flash and Instamatic.

Rhythmically controlled and coherent, the first couplet bodes well, but already in the second there is an overload which results in a clumpy rhythm and the ungainly pseudo-rhyme. In 'H' prisoners in the H-Block are up in arms about issues relating to sausage rolls. Having determined at the outset to cast his poem in rhymed couplets, Carson then seems to be struggling against them with the prose rhythm of:

> The prisoners complained. We cannot reproduce his actual
>   words here, since their spokesman is alleged
> To be a sub-commander of a movement deemed to be illegal.

However, there are marvellous touches as he plays with the ideas of shibboleths and territory:

> Well, give an inch and someone takes an effing mile. Every
>   thing is in the ways
> You say them. Like, the prison that we call Long Kesh is to
>   the Powers-that-Be *The Maze*.

Ultimately, though, the poems are written to a formula and too often seem merely to serve as a vehicle for Carson's erudition, so that poetry is reduced to the status of a crossword puzzle. One either 'gets' the references, jokes, whatever, or one doesn't, but is not always convinced that it really matters.

In 1998, only two years after the appearance of *Opera Et Cetera,* Carson brought out two new volumes. The first, *The Alexandrine Plan,* is a collection of 34 sonnets freely adapted from Baudelaire, Rimbaud, and Mallarmé. This was followed soon after by *The Twelfth of Never,* a collection of 77 original sonnets written in alexandrines, the standard line of French verse. Thus, the collection has a formal unity, but unlike *Opus Et Cetera* it also has a thematic unity as Carson deconstructs the idea of history in general, but Irish history in particular, creating his own mythology of a 'Never Never Land':

> There is a green hill far away, without a city wall,
> Where cows have longer horns than any that we know;
> Where daylight hours behold a moon of indigo,
> And fairy cobblers operate without an awl.

This is a world of fairy tales and riddling ballads. It is also a world of paradoxes 'Ruled by Zeno's eternal tortoises and hares / Where everything is metaphor and simile.' In 'The Rising of the Moon', the title of which is borrowed from a ballad referring to the 1798 rebellion in County Wexford, we find ourselves in a more specifically Irish context:

> As down by the glenside I met an old colleen,
> She stung me with the gaze of her nettle green eyes,
> She urged me to go out and revolutionize
> Hibernia, and not to fear the Guillotine.

The protagonist then finds himself amongst the downtrodden 'People of No Property', Carson's ironic twist on 'No Popery', the rallying call of the Protestant ascendancy. Over the page 'The Rising of the Moon' is followed by 'The Rising Sun', a poem in which he transports us to ' smoky Tokyo', a strange parallel universe where the yen 'had been going down / All day against the buoyant Hibernian Pound'. In 'The Groves of Blarney', another poem which shares its title with a traditional Irish song, it is not entirely clear whether Carson is sending up the blarney or is himself milking it:

> 'Tis there you'll find the woods of shamrock and shillelagh
> And the pratie gardens full of Easter snow;
> You'll hear the blackbird sing a gay risorgimento,
> And see Venus rising at the dawning of the day.

Unfortunately, for all its high jinks *The Twelfth of Never* is, like *Opus Et*

Cetera, a disappointing collection. After a while the folksy rhythms become monotonous and much of the imagery is repetitive. While Carson's use of the alexandrine may be ambitious it is not entirely successful. French is a very different, more lightly stressed language than English, and Carson's attempt to adopt its prosody to English leads frequently to rhythms that are tired and flat, reminding one of Alexander Pope's famous description of the alexandrine 'That, like a wounded snake, drags its slow length along.'

In little more than a decade between the years 1987-1998 Carson produced five substantial collections, three of which placed him in the front rank of contemporary poets. It would be another five years before his next collection appeared. When in 2003 he published *Breaking News* it marked another watershed and saw Carson abandoning his long lines for a Creeleyesque brevity. In an explanatory note to the collection he also acknowledges his indebtedness to the Anglo-Irish journalist William Henry Russell, whom he cites as being 'generally regarded as the father of the art of war correspondence' and who made his name by his dispatches from the Crimean War. In *Breaking News* there is not a trace of that highly wrought allusiveness which for so long had been Carson's signature as he aims now for the immediacy and the visual impact of reportage. The poems mark not only a return to the Belfast of the Troubles, but also turn their gaze to that earlier conflict in the Crimea, whose key battles are memorialized in many of the city's street names. There is also a long poem on the Indian Mutiny and, symptomatic of the new primacy he gives to the visual as opposed to the auditory, there are poems on paintings by the artists Goya, Géricault, and Hopper.

In 'Belfast', his wonderfully astringent opening poem, it's as if Carson is rediscovering the uncluttered directness of his first collection:

east

beyond the yellow
shipyard cranes

a blackbird whistles
in a whin bush

west

beside the motorway
a black taxi

rusts in a field
of blue thistles

Informed by Carson's love of early Irish poetry and the Japanese *haiku*, this piece manages to encapsulate a thousand years of Irish history from its iconic image of the blackbird to the notorious associations of the Belfast black taxi. 'The Gladstone Bar circa 1954' is another poem that would not have been out of place in *The New Estate:* 'two men are / unloading beer // you can smell / the hops and yeast // the smouldering / heap of dung // just dropped by / one / of the great / blinkered drayhorses'. After his seemingly exhaustive coverage of Belfast's streets in earlier collections one might imagine that it would be difficult for Carson to write much more about them, but like a good photo-journalist his eye misses nothing, not even a damaged shop sign in 'News': 'alarms / shrill // lights / flash // as dust / clears // above / the paper // shop // *The Belfast Telegraph* / sign reads // *fast* // *rap*'.

Moving from Belfast to the Crimea, 'War' is a grisly footnote to Tennyson's 'The Charge of The Light Brigade': 'Sergeant Talbot / had his head // swept off // by a // round-shot // yet for half / a furlong // more // the body kept / the saddle // horse and rider / charging on // regardless'; whilst in 'Campaign' it is hard to imagine how anyone could capture more successfully in less than twenty words the futility of war and nature's indifference to it:

shot
the horse fell

a crow
plucked the eyes

time passed

from a socket
crept

a butterfly

Finally, *The Collected Poems* is brought to a close by Carson's 2008 collection *For All We Know*. A technical tour de force and perhaps the most formally perfect work of poetry that Carson has produced, its anatomy of love and separation is moving to a degree which transcends its virtuosity. The book is divided into two sequences of 35 poems. The title of each poem in the first half is repeated in the same order in the second. Each poem is written in unrhymed couplets of 14, 21, or 42 lines and each line has 14 syllables. Miraculously, there is no sense of strain as through this maze of sinuous and burnished lines Carson evokes a love affair between an Irishman, Gabriel, and a Frenchwoman, Nina. Moving beyond the narrative techniques first developed in *The Irish for No,* the story expands to the length of a short novel and has to be pieced together from hints and shifting memories which are reminiscent of the uncertainties of the *nouveau roman,* most particularly that lyrical obsessiveness one finds in the novels of Marguerite Duras.

Moreover, like Duras in *Moderato Cantabile,* and as so often before in Carson's work, the book is partly inspired by music. In an epigraph to the collection he quotes Glenn Gould's 'So you want to write a fugue?' 'Fugue must perform its frequently stealthy work with continuously shifting melodic fragments that remain in the "tune sense" perpetually unfinished'. Carson also emphasises the elegiac nature of his tale by prefacing it with a scrap of French song: 'Night approaches and my village / slumbers over there in silence / The bell rings and its language / Announces the end of farewells' (Carson's translation).

From the outset it is not only the reader but the protagonists themselves who are dogged by uncertainty as they try to make sense of a relationship that is complicated by linguistic and cultural differences:

> I was grappling
> with your language over the wreck of the dining table.
>
> The maitre d' was looking at us in a funny way
> as if he caught the drift I sought between the lines you spoke.
>
> For one word never came across as just itself, but you
> would put it over as insinuating something else.
>
> Then slowly, slowly we would draw in on one another
> until everything was implicated like wool spooled
>
> from my yawning hands as you wound the yarn into a ball.
> For how many seasons have we circled round each other
>
> like this? Was it because you came from there and I came from here?

One senses, too, in 'On the Contrary' that although the relationship is haunted by the lovers' separate pasts, it may also offer them a means of escape:

It's because we were brought up to lead double lives, you said.
You were lying next to me, both of us verging on sleep.

We always had to withhold ourselves from the other side,
guarding our tongues lest we answer to their outspoken laws.

And so we lost ourselves in the dark forest of language
believing in nothing which might not be governed by touch

or taste, the apple bursting indescribably with juice
against the roof of the mouth, or the clean cold smell of skin.

Gradually, as the narrative ranges across Paris, Belfast, Dresden and Berlin it takes on the atmosphere of a *roman noir*, evoking memories of the Cold War and further back to the Nazi occupation of France. In 'Shadow' there is a meeting with a former *Stasi* agent who explains the difference between truth and lies: 'You know how you know when someone's telling lies? ... They / get their story right every time... // Whereas when they tell the truth it's never the same twice... // ...they sometimes ask themselves if it happened at all.' In 'Je Reviens' we learn that the affaire ends in tragedy and see then in 'Zugzwang' how Gabriel must struggle endlessly to make sense of it all:

as the quilters make a pattern of their remnants and rags,
and the jersey, unravelled, becomes a new skein of wool;

as the fugue must reiterate its melodic fragments
in continuously unfinished tapestries of sound [...]

so I return to the question of these staggered repeats
as my memories of you recede unto the future.

For All we Know is a fitting and triumphant conclusion to Carson's *Collected Poems*. Characterised by its consummate artistry, it shows him again breaking new ground, whilst at the same time it resonates with echoes of earlier work such as the image of the patchwork quilt, which first appeared in his pamphlet *The Lost Explorer*. A poet who is constantly driven by his need to reinvent himself, there seems to be little he can't do with language. The iconic poet of Belfast throughout the darkest period of its recent history, he is now, by virtue of his technical brilliance and the depth and range of his emotional impact, one of the most accomplished poets writing in English today.

W S Milne

Fleur Adcock's Classicism

Unlike many contemporary poets, Fleur Adcock possesses deep roots in the western classical tradition of literature. She has the classicist's disposition and training, 'the Greek blue' of antiquity as she terms it, a crafted, considered art catching more than just a passing mood. Her outlook strikes the 'necessary balance' between tradition and originality, fusing the old and the new. Her poems are intimate compositions concerned with personal matters, after the manner of Sappho:

> Walking about from room to room
> to find the source of all this moonlight…
>
> and there it is, in front of the house,
> not even halfway around it yet
> but shining full and flat into my eyes;
> (not much past 3A.M., it turns out);
> and I am still a day off 70.

(from 'An Observation,' in Dragon Talk)

From the beginning (from the first poem, 'Note on Propertius,' in her first collection, *The Eye of the Hurricane*, 1964) Adcock has always kept ancient models in mind: not the traditional arch of epic, nor the masculine lines of Ionic or Corinthian capitals, but portraits of real women and real men in real places, suffering bare, unembellished lives and deaths. In her satire on Propertius, for instance, she overturns the stilted male panegyric to love, demolishing conventional marble nymphs and ornamental urns to replace them with Cynthia's perspective, vistas which include 'a sallowed moon' and love's 'spiny flesh.' A woman's everyday pain, her anxiety, is introduced to subvert male romantic fustian, and to provoke a fresh response in the reader. She turns such tropes as Catullus' 'What a woman says to her eager lover should be / Written in wind and in swirling water,' and his 'Let her go and get on with it with those lechers of hers' (in Robin Nisbet's translations) on their head by using the tradition *against* men:

> I would not have you drain
> with your sodden lips the flesh that has fed on mine,

and leech his bubbling blood to a decline:
not that pain;

nor visit on his mind
that other desiccation, where the wit
shrivels: so to be humbled is not fit
for his kind.

But use acid or flame,
secretly, to brand or cauterise;
and on the soft globes of his mortal eyes
etch my name.

('Instructions to Vampires,' in *Tigers*,1967)

(It is as if one heard Deborah singing of Jael, wife of Heber, driving a tent-peg through Sisera's brow, or were witnessing Judith cutting off Holofernes' head!) The tone is an aggressive development of Elizabeth Barrett Browning's 'Lord Walter's Wife': 'You take us for harlots, I tell you, and not for the women we are.' It is a very strong form of secular lyricism.

We can see something more of this particular contempt, or scorn, in her translations from the Greek epigrammatist Marcus Argentarius:

About Menophila's morals there are strange rumours:
They say her mouth, to astronomers, can provide
An image of heaven: under one small roof
The sword of Orion, with room for the Twins beside.

(from *The Greek Anthology*, 1973)

The difference here is that Argentarius (a man) finds Menophila's manners revolting, whilst Adcock (a woman) celebrates the Greek woman's sexual freedom and liberation. Once again, the tradition is used as a weapon of female riposte. Here we have the *archetypus* for such famous poems of Adcock's as 'Against Coupling,' 'The Ex-Queen Among the Astronomers,' 'Instructions to Vampires,' 'Incident,' 'Advice to a Discarded Lover' and 'Madmen,' and all those fine poems concerned with the phantasmagoria of nightmare, the Hieronymus Bosch-like hell of:

I see myself inspecting the vast slit
of a sagging whore; making love with a hunchbacked
hermaphrodite; eating worms or shit;

67

or rapt upon necrophily or incest...

(from 'Mornings After,' in *High Tide in the Garden*, 1971)

– all those dreams that drag us down to the deep, peopled with monsters.

But there is a softer side to Adcock, a more playful one, and it is very much to the fore in *Dragon Talk*:

> When he jumped on you (at this point the pronoun
> bifurcates from dual to singular),
> my fellow female, he was off in a second.
> You quivered with astonishment for minutes.
>
> You definitely preferred the foreplay –
> the chocolates and champagne, as it were;
> in view of which, accept my platonic
> offering: a bowl of little wrigglers.

(from 'To the Robins')

This tender tone has more in common with the other Greek epigrammatists that she has translated, Leonidas and Agathias, for example, and in particular the female poet Moiro:

> Now you lie – a grape-offering,
> A severed cluster, a bag of wine-juice –
> In Aphrodite's gilded porch.
> Never again will the vine your mother
> Curl her kindly branch about you
> Or spread over your head her scented leaves.

(from *The Greek Anthology*)

Her translations give the tradition a new bite, a new freshness and vigour. It is the same tenderness we see in such poems as 'For Andrew', 'Instead of an Interview,' and 'House-Talk.' An Apollonian tone sustains *Dragon Talk*. The earlier Dionysian frenzy has settled down to a gentler quietness:

It's true about the butterfly –
a peacock, no common tortoiseshell –
that surged in through the open window.

You were in your coffin in New Zealand.
I was here, in my hot London study,
trying to get my voice to work

as Marilyn held the telephone
over your dead face. You couldn't wait:
you fluttered in at once to comfort me.

You were no showy beauty, dear mother,
but your personality was bright rainbow,
and your kindness had velvety wings.

   The best of Fleur Adcock's work is often epigrammatic (see, for example, 'Briddes,' 'Pupation,' 'Coupling,' 'The Drought Breaks,' and 'Skype'), intelligent, passionately precise, with sharp powers of observation:

Half and hour before my flight was called
he walked across the airport bar towards me
carrying what was left of our future
together: two drinks on a tray.

('Send-off,' in The Inner Harbour, 1979)

This is what she calls her 'laconic style,' her 'little package of words,' the poem pared down to the minimum for maximum effect. It is a quality, or strength, evident in her longer poems as well where the impact of a single sentence or a phrase can be devastating: 'Gone is gone forever' (akin to Catullus' *nox est perpetua una dormienda*), 'What wanted to be said is said,' 'It was hard to work out what to resent,' 'When I woke up that morning I had no father,' 'I , by your example, am well-schooled in contempt,' 'The first transvestite I ever went to bed with,' 'all my scars are yours,' 'What passion ever inspired a sloth to mate?', 'Let's be clear about this: I love toads,' 'watching the bright wind attack the ice,' and so on. This vivid economy in her writing has all the pithiness and balance of the Classical Mean, the Via Media. H. D. F. Kitto (in *The Greeks*) has written that 'The Mean did not imply the absence of tension and lack of passion, but the correct tension which gives out the true and clear note,' the avoidance of bombast. It is just such a note that we hear in Fleur Adcock's poetry. A whole intellectual-emotional complex is set out with clarity in a single poem or sentence with an exactness, subtlety and humour demonstrating a command of situation:

> On the wall above the bedside lamp
> a large crane-fly is jump-starting
> a smaller crane-fly – or vice versa.
> They do it tail to tail, like Volkswagens:
> their engines must be in their rears.
>
> It looks easy enough. Let's try it.

This is the whole of the poem entitled 'Coupling,' from the 1991 volume, *Time-Zones,* and exemplifies her erotic, racy, demotic, imagistic, punchy style at its best. It serves as a companion-piece to her notorious poem on female masturbation of 1971, 'Against Coupling' (from *High Tide in the Garden*). It is here, in this type of contrast, this balance, that we see Adcock's classicism at its clearest, not wishing to be cast down on one side of the scales only. The Greeks worshipped Aphrodite *and* Artemis (Love *and* Virtue, if you like) on the same level. To be obsessed with one at the expense of the other would have been deemed madness. A Marquis de Sade or a St Simeon Stylites would have been unimaginable to them (although Diogenes approaches the extreme at times, it is true). And so it is in Adcock's world: there is a place for solitariness and a place for socialising, a time to love and a time to hate, an occasion to admire and an occasion to scorn. One would hardly be human if one did not live in such a crux of ambiguities, of lovers' 'ludicrous violence in kitchens,' of tenderness in bed, of mothers lying to their children to console them, of self-loathing ('the razor-marks at wrist and elbow'), of unreserved love ('little pink mouths touched / Like foxglove-bells over my nipples'), and of the humour that can lie even in illness:

> Nellie has only one breast
> ample enough to make several.

> (from 'The Soho Hospital for Women,' in *The Inner Harbour*)

(One can hardly imagine a man making such a quip!) There are 'so many tones' in life she says, 'one can't be sure of one's reading.' Such a philosophy necessarily entails a rational balance in life, a secure fulcrum ensuring sanity.

Fleur Adcock scours male territory to bring back rich female spoils, destroying male-centredness in the process, and tearing off the masks of male chivalry and politeness, overthrowing accepted proprieties and female reticence:

> It is the long grass that is so erotic...
>   inviting us
> to cling together, fall, roll into it
> blind and gasping, smothered by stalks and hair,
> pollen and each other's tongues on our hot faces...
>
> We walk a yard apart, talking
> of literature and botany.
> We have known each other, remotely, for nineteen years.

(from 'Prelude,' in The Inner Harbour)

Adcock's poetry has been particularly influential among younger women poets (one thinks especially of Carol Ann Duffy, for instance), and one intimates that they owe much to her matter-of-fact realism. She is audacious and innovative, as Sappho herself was, and one can imagine a modern pope, if he had the power, condemning her works to be burned as both Gregory Nazianzen and Gregory VII did Sappho's in 380 and in 1073 respectively. There are times, it is true, when she is wary of poetry's attractions, its 'honeyed gift,' its 'golden frame' of art; she writes of 'the treacheries of the word,' that 'there are other gods besides the muses,' and of 'a late quartet which would also save us from nothing,'– but again, on the other side, she can write, for balance, of poetry's 'sweet symmetry', that 'in the end we have literature to salve our wounds.'

There is a strong current of Epicureanism in Adcock's work, and it is evident still in *Dragon Talk*, although the pleasures seem more muted now. In the earlier work we have an emphasis on 'the long-necked bottle,' 'the wine-jar,' the blessings of smoking, 'the god Priapus,' of 'giving Aphrodite and Bacchus a chance,' of 'taking your pleasures whole,' 'the sweet obvious act' of sex, of 'a conspiracy of our bodies,' all the 'senses operative,' letting the breeze, in one poem, provocatively 'blow up my nightdress,' celebrating *uoluptas*, the 'throb,' the 'hard spurt,' the 'passionate rise' of love. We see her enjoying the sensuous pleasures of house-painting and of washing the sheets after making love (a detail no man would take stock of, that is for certain), of watching slugs making love, and of being delivered of 'the slimy surprise' of a baby. Such an open, unsentimental perspective is very invigorating and radical ('Ah, acceptance!' she says at one point, 'leave me under this stone.') It is certainly far removed from 'the dreamy rose' (as she calls it) of love's tradition. The pleasures now are more to do with being a grandmother, as in 'A Garland for Rosa':

> Dear Rosa, twenty years before I knew
> that one day there might be someone like you
> I planted this: a rose with which you share
> part of your name – as also with 'the Fair
> Rosamund'; the rose of the world it means...

Dragon Talk continues themes taken up in *Looking Back* (1997) and *New Poems* (2000). In all three volumes we find an emphasis on the beauties of the natural world, of a quick sensitiveness to wildlife, of the threats to the environment, of chemical and nuclear weapons, of radioactive rain, of endangered flora and fauna, a picture of humankind 'gobbling the world'. She writes with the keenness of a naturalist (one of her favourite authors is the great French entomologist, Henri Fabre), of 'the wild arum lilies,' 'the dunnocks,' 'the housemartins,' and 'the thrushes.' 'The dreamy abstract stare' of the theorist does not interest her, only the naturalist's love of 'the loamy scent,' what she succinctly calls her 'love affair with the natural world.' Hers is an 'Earth-based, earth-bound' poetry with a sustained care and interest in all the ephemera, and again these concerns are evident in *Dragon Talk*, in poems such as 'A Rose Tree,' 'Miramar,' 'The Mill Stream,' 'the Table,' 'Casein,' and in 'Linseed.'

Transience has been a theme in her work from the start, from the translations in *The Greek Anthology* on:

> Dead, you will lie under a yard of earth,
> Far from daylight and all delighting.
> So drain the cup; take your pleasures whole;
> Embrace that beautiful girl, your wife;
> And pin no hopes on 'immortal wisdom':
> Cleanthes and Zeno lie as deep as any.

(after Marcus Argentarius)

We find her writing of 'the gradual running down of the film,' of mortality's 'sudden earth and sun,' of death's 'last cold fury,' its 'clutching gravity,' its 'deep flower opening,' its 'fell flood' and 'ungentle music.' The elegies to James K. Baxter (in *The Scenic Route*), to Pete Laver ('The Keepsake,' in *The Incident Book*, 1986), and to Fiona Lodge ('The Farm,' in *Time-Zones*) are particularly moving and memorable, as indeed is the one to her mother in *Dragon Talk* (quoted above). 'The black cypress stalks after us all' she says, in Horatian mode (Horace, whom she elsewhere chides as 'the timid enjoyer,' 'Horace, / on whom the dreaded tree never did quite fall'). 'Outside the Crematorium,' in *Dragon Talk*, takes us back to the unexpected side-views of 'The Soho Hospital for Women' of *The Inner Harbour*:

> The sun is shining calmly. I could almost
> get used to this death business – except
>
> that our last funeral was for a baby,
> whose grandmother has just been telling us
> how she helped to wash and dress her for it,
> and how hard it was to get her vest on.

So it is that what the Psalmist calls 'the dust of death' is ever present in her poetry.

In *Dragon Talk* we have poems concerned with a war-time childhood spent as an evacuee in Leicestershire, Wiltshire and Kent, the poet seeking out her family ties in the North, the Fens and the Midlands, writing of her first ball, her wedding, writing her first letter, bombing raids, rationing, her father in ARP overalls, the Morrison shelter in the garden, of the émigré's life in Tunbridge Wells, Frant and Sidcup, and vignettes of a grandmother (herself) keeping up with the new technology. This reflection on the past reminds us of earlier glimpses, of the exile's loneliness in the metropolis, in 'a bed lousy with dreams,' in the psychiatrist's 'formal chair,' recognising the 'centrelessness' of her own being at the same time as praising her inner 'watchdog,' her self-sufficiency and self-reliance (telling one lover, adamantly, 'You needn't think I am here to stay'); poems on her travels to New Zealand, London, Newcastle upon Tyne, Romania, Nepal, Ireland and The Lake District, a comprehensive sketch-book of cosmopolitan impressions.

Lucretius' inventive earth is at the fore in this latest collection also, abounding in flowers and beasts, demonstrating a comprehensive sympathy with universal nature. Adcock observes the inner rationale of nature not with a Swiftian disgust but with an uncluttered directness, not wanting to ignore the true nature of things. In this she is classical to the core. In generating a wide imaginative vista, of 'garlands,' 'tokens,' 'emblems' and 'icons,' the poet sees things as they are, and not as we would wish them to be. We have in her work a clear Aristotelian outlook, a love of natural detail as fecund as that of Marianne Moore's or of Elizabeth Bishop's. As in the best of Greek art, amongst 'the clogging multiplicity of things' as she calls it, the dust and din of the world, Adcock establishes a central truth: that women stand equal to men. In her poems of a passionate and erotic life we discover a woman who does not think love coterminous with life, giving the lie to all those men, from Propertius through Lord Byron and on, who think otherwise, a poet who mercilessly anatomises men's arrogance and violence. Romantic love is contrasted with 'the hairy den' of its reality (the phrase recalls Ruskin's horror at the sight of his wife's pubic hair on their wedding night), the beast with 'the fangs, the eyes, the bristling ears,' the whole clash of innocence with experience. Adcock shows a woman can outmatch a man in lover's venom, or outdo him in contempt. She lampoons men's traditional patronising of supposed 'feminine qualities' (such as softness, beauty, gentleness, and so on) and candidly emancipates women from such clichéd shackles. Although she may rely on traditional elements, her poetry adds something new to literature. Poetry's 'mute inscription' will triumph over any loud 'performance':

> And what was the happiest day I remember?
> It was when we went to the Mill Stream –
>
> my sister and I and the Morris kids.
> We wore our bathing-suits under our dresses
>
> (subterfuge), crossed the live railway lines
> (forbidden), and tramped through bluebell woods.
>
> There was a bridge with green and brown shadows
> to lurk among in the long afternoon...

> (from 'The Mill Stream,' in *Dragon Talk*)

Such idyllic, tender moments even out the instances of spleen and revenge.
   The whole of her poetry is very human and very real in its balance, and demonstrates a learned classicism re-invented for modern times.

Alyson Hallett

Clark's Shoe Factory

What I wanted was the factory
before it turned into a shopping village.
Wanted the Henry Moore sheep piece
back on the grass by the factory tower,
wanted the hum of sewing machines
and that dusty smell of leather. Wanted
to cycle past the stinking tannery,
to walk in wear-test shoes, to eat the cakes
at Clark's Christmas party. Not nostalgia,
but a wanting for things that made us.
The workers' dirty hands, the day
after day, the doughnuts in the canteen.
My father going up and down Street
High Street for more than forty years.
The fact that things were being made,
the attraction of that. The grit and the skill
and the boredom. I wanted to see it all again.
To know the cut of cow hide, the stitch,
the moulded sole of a shoe. Not the museum
but the living practice. The meaning
of that brick high up in the factory wall
with the words *more light* carved into it.

Dear Dream Doctor,

night after night I still dream of him
as if all the years of separation
(how many is it now, twenty,
twenty two, twenty three?)
count for nothing. There have been
other lives, other lovers,
but still he appears with the same face,
the same voice, as if the needle
of choicelessness that stitched us together once
still stitches us together now.
Reliable as the rituals of breakfast,
dinner, tea, he comes to me –
what keeps him there? In this country
that can never be mapped?
There was no thought back then
of the sentence I might
be destined to serve: love old as stars
and just as inextinguishable. Dear
dream doctor, what am I failing
to see and do you know if
he spends night after night
dreaming of me?

John F. Deane

Dusk

It was April, but a late March hare was shadow-boxing
with the evening moon,
there, on our front lawn; I envied him, big bucko, my sweet
latchiko, his out-there

otherness and plantedness, the phrase *hoc erat in principio*
hanging on my mind.
High in branches of the ash trees, finches and chiffchaffs
chorused, a team of long-tailed tits

came by to scold the big-limbed loper, who sat, quietened now,
priest-like on our grass. He sat alert,
some moments of composure in the good air, land lord
and local hero, his living

close to the bone, in a certain low-mass, sacramental
intensity, lest there be
fox-eyes widening from a covert or the baleful muzzle of a shotgun
poking from a hide;

he moved, mincingly at first, then sped, surefooted and at ease
back into his secrecies,
leaving me in confirmation with the earth, glad that I could face
the going down of the sun in sacred company.

Shelf-Life

From a side-hook in the pantry, Old Moore's
Almanac for 1943, its pages browned from the pipe-smoke
of Grandpa Time, and one china cup without its handles,
a small blue boat drifting towards the bridge; one   -

Knock-shrine mug, repository for two brass keys
that have lost their locks; a brawn-coloured oval
roasting-dish, its cracked-over surface criss-crossed
with the trackways of old Europe; a Rowntree's Cocoa tin,

its comely maiden watching out onto hurrying time
with a face of wonder; a carriage-clock without its hands,
standing in its final after-tock; Hallow-e'en tin rings
without their lustre; a Brigid's Cross, the rushes dried

brittle as old wicks; and there, in a cardboard box,
the mixed-up bits of Lego, Meccano, jigsaws, those
building blocks of a world to be. Two off-green, birthday
balloons, wrinkled and out-of-breath, string still knotted

like scarves on their scrawny necks, and there, on the top shelf
my tin-ware porringer from lunch-time school, long emptied
of my peaceful indifference to all things. Finally, me, here
mooching about in my ghosthood over shelves no longer there.

John Clare's Bedlam

What do they pack for you in that battered suitcase
as they leave you to the madhouse door? How do they say

'goodbye'? how turn away? And how do you
turn from them, from the finches, from the sloe-

blossoms and music of the rainclouds – how do you face
towards that scanting cell? How will the warm sun's rays

discover where you are, all this not in the scheme
of God's devising? Can you sing while you suffer the severe

processes they have planned for your purgation?
– bleedings, chemicals – to turn the runnels of your brain

to oozings? And all the while the unfazed robin
calls you to rake for her the good, black earth again,

the fox would lead you down his trodden path, through
fragrances of pine, the tough-branched undergrowth you know

out to the heather marches where you would hymn, apart,
God and made-things, Christ and abundance, because the heart

is a shire too great to be enclosed, and the sky above is chaste
and shiftful as divinity, life-giving as the dark blood of the Christ.

Tim Liardet

from *The Storm House*

The only piece of action in the dream was the opening of the window, of its own accord;
for the wolves sat quite still and without making any movement in the branches of the
tree, to the right and left of the trunk, and looked at him. There were six or seven of
them. It seemed as though they had riveted their whole attention on him.

Sigmund Freud, *From the History of an Infantile Neurosis, 1918*

14

There were many journeys, there were half-journeys,
but that of the heart a pilgrimage in reverse,
a return to the source from which to set out again.
World conspired, as always, lamp-posts buckled
your bonnet and engine, trees moved into your head-lamps;
you wooed danger only so you could return
to the chair shaped to your comfort, opposite our mother.
At twenty, as at fifty, you knew the ritual so well
there might have been marks for your elbow
and one for the placing of your foot, a pot
for your keys by the door—as if all the words
you could not speak out loud were written
in a letter slid beneath the only brick
in the whole house that was loose, rueing your luck.

Such lights as burn in the hotel, our mother's convinced,
attract you still. In death as in life, she says,
the old reverberations reach her. The flash-lamps bob
at the window, and your face is behind them;
your eye is at the peep-hole and magnified
twice its size, so blue—your fingers at the letter box.
In an apartment shuttered by dark glass,
she says, she follows the sounds through the wall
while each of those porcelain clowns you bought for her
holds up an instrument and farded look
as if playing a tune no one else but you can hear.
Faced with this disturbance which shakes
more than her pot of pins, you understand, I put on in my head
Tchaikovsky's *Danse Russe*, and turn it up loud.

24

Imagine the act of love, or will, which swings back
in a single lunging motion the heartbreaking distance
to the inch between nose and nose—yours and hers.
In this cycle, it seems, she has mistaken
darkness for daylight, and daylight for dark.
If one reveals to her the dew on spider silks
spot-lit by a low trajectory, the other draws up to her chin
a duck-quilt of unseeing. And they might
change places, they might pose as one another.
If I am the one who feels you watching me
and imagines you passing – like a spider on the stairs –
our mother's been reported missing from herself
and cannot quite trace back all that's been mislaid;
or what it is that has, or has not been said.

26

The spooks, the offices of the dead, the stink
of the Chapel's lilies drifting from room to room
like a mild gas, the hole you have left which sets
the few who survive you hurrying to form
alliances that are new—all of these a single smell,
an atmosphere, the sort of chill which creeps
but cannot weight the hems of the few frenetic seconds
of Pyotr Illyich's thirty violins in full flight
free-riding me to joy, the spring and leap
of energy suddener than body and world:
now that I must see for two, I must attempt also
to live the life I owe you and find a way to clog-dance,
to jitterbug, to tap or otherwise to jig
on the brilliant ice that is your coffin lid.

27

Imagine all of it, brother, set to such music. The years
of bitterness, your death, the drama of your return
or of your never-having-left—out of sinc;
the music, the events, glancing off each other.
The truth is you died with a hole in your shoe
through to your foot, without socks, like poor Dylan
found between the last turning of Eleventh Street
and Saint Luke's in The Field, you on our own bed:
his shoes were worn through the contours to a hole
and a few grains of Laugharne sand, yours
to no grains at all, no love of place nor of anything.
What you shared was a lonely end with similar stuff
boiling in your antibodies—the both of you lost
in the city of self which towered, awaiting the first frost.

29

You wanted to be feared in life for the silo
of your own body, you wanted to have been born
of lesser blood and have straining from one fist
your grim succession of powerful dogs:
something of the wolf in them, the mouth from which
the tongue gagged like a piston on the move
and the breadth of chest and muscle-yoke
drew you down into them, or dragged you along
until it was in question who led the way.
You threw them commands that were thrown through you
but I can recall how once an albedo mist
cast a strange sort of light across your smile
and filled your whole mouth, which was lowered
as if it had never once spoken a word.

32

You know the turnings beyond the world
that have never been mapped, the pathos of the last street lamp
getting smaller and smaller. You know the truth
of how light divides, how the world slips through
the finest division of light, and is gone.
You know the terror of the peacock which
legs it across the lawn, as the first drops of a million gallons
bounce a leaf, then another—this is how it begins.
The snarl is gone. The flood in the lane will gather
to overwhelm its defences and pick up silt
and the night release new mineral smells
which are cleaner and newer, fresher and more green:
water is air, earth water. Air is fire, and the fire
of water's getting hungry for its reservoir.

Andrew McNeillie

Lead kindly light

Insomniac the night itself, out there for company.
The tanker constellations ride in the bay,
waiting for the pilot, for guidance, and burn
a beauty not their own but the gazer's longing
and thought of seven seas and far-flung ports.
Someone out there like me keeping watch
looks ashore at the ribbons of street lights,
the dock's fire of arc-lamps, over the hill,
a ghost of hotel fronts and flash of tidemark.
If the pilot boat would come now, the ferry,
dawn would not be far round the headland.

But the night is young and revelling home
with wave-cavortings and mirror-shadows,
urban music on a beer-can and shark-violence
down backstreets and drownings of the heart.
The country of deeper shadow folds itself
in to itself and sleeps through mere flotsam
of the human tide, signs of the times,
jetsam to go, the way of all things soon enough,
the World Service talking to itself of bad times
and good works where the hungry listen
to the paper-thin myths from imperial London.

Peace and rest elude me. My strategy
to read, to scribble, and restlessly to prowl
parting the curtain to stare at the rail-halt
blowing and deserted and a tall cut-out pine
blacker than night, in this alien corner of a new life,
reminding me of somewhere else that once
held my heart with a passion. Lead kindly
light I murmur where I lie, and for revelation
pilot myself to unconsciousness at last,
thinking as I sink, that it's too late again,
as the present escapes me into the light.

Elegy

I want to put you out to grass, set
you aside, and leave you fallow.

For you to winter an aeon or two
and watch time pass without regret.

Wallflower

I never wanted to, but put me through it
I did, imagining my shyness to be
undecided, and sometimes finding pity.
But I look askance at them now and all that
marriage has entailed, for those forward
blooms who couldn't bear to be ignored.

James Simpson

from *The Untenanted Room*

i

We have come to this place
where we kill all gods and dreams,
something inconsequential
we scribble in the margin of our lives.

We write words, but words lie forgotten,
throats are cut, voices taken
and in a glance of life
we trample everything underfoot,
scrabbling to reach the chamber door.

Where oh where is the greenstick boy?
Who has heard the night bird's song?
Even the frosts are gone and the old grain
does not seem to grow anymore.

vi

Sift, sift my love
and take a snatch of honey
in your mouth.

The bees come to suckle you,
husk upon little husk,
it is a mean breath they offer.

Shh, there are no flowers
bless the rain on summer bowers,
let me tear each leaf in three

to twine around my fingers;
bind and unbind to find an end,
this the art to which I pretend.

Lullay, lullay my little liking
let me cradle you in this shroud
like a leveret in his coffin.

ix

A thin place in a thin time,
the blood bracked shuddering
in all the glass night;
and we the taut marchers and frost merriers
clasped onto earth's compass
and the crest capped haunches;
singing nights' crystal
and the ward welled blessing.

Through night's branches, gleaming
like starlings, over hillsides
and the breast papped chalk-lands,
lighted like candles and guttering torches.
Ours is the singing of the antlers blazing,
ours is the claim of the boar tusk whittling,
freeing the midden of the oak tree island,
singing the night and the unforgetting.

xii

I have marked the dead seasons
one by one;
heard footfalls fall again,
fall in a night

so dark, that hills and sky
were one in sound
and still; but for the unusual air
twisting in the beech leaves.

What mysteries are these?
This mouthpiece uttering
the moon's limed walls.

Honest tongue,
there is nothing to be said:
this is the time of candle care
when frost lays
bitter the partial ground;

the lark has spun
the world on its axis
and the blood
we have shed is mutual.

David Cooke

At Varykino

You insist upon living till the life
you'd live has damned you, your intransigence
forcing you on like a train that pounds
its rhythms across some hard white terrain.

Adulterous and anachronistic, a stubborn
glow illuminates your doomed *affaire*
as when, like a ghost reborn, Strelnikov
told you the private life is dead;

his rectitude a new kind of purity
whose thought is doctrinaire,
his speech a bridled mob of precepts
that makes you seek your chances

beyond the margin of events.
Arriving at Varykino, you find a house
that is wrecked in snow, a past's discredited
chattels forgotten beneath its sheets.

There is no sense beyond gesture
as you rework the pattern
of days stripped of consequence, awaiting spring,
its new growth pushing beneath untrodden snow.

Shadow-Boxing

The closest my dad ever got to poetry
was when he savoured some word
like *pugilist*, or the tip-toe springiness
he sensed in *bob and weave*,
his unalloyed delight in the flytings
and eyeball to eyeball hype
that went with big fight weigh-ins.

And I, too, might have been
a contender when I did my stint
in the ring, my dad convinced
I had the style and stamp of a winner,
when in the end I just got bored.
You had to have a killer's instinct,
to do much better than a draw.

In the gym the lights are low.
It's after hours. I'm on my own.
The boards are rank with sweat
and stale endeavour. Shadow-boxing
like the best of them, I will show
him feints, a classic stance,
trying always to keep up my guard.

.

Gary Allen

The Boxer

My father would never let me do boxing –
and I hated him for that.
I would see the other boys come out of the red brick club house
behind the Parochial Hall, smoking half butts
worn leather gloves hanging around their necks

the lights of the halls burning away the winter gloom
the ropes hanging from the low ceiling
the suspended punch bags
the torn posters –
the stink of the blocked drains.

The trainer worked in the local butcher shop,
Why don't you call up? he would say
on Saturday mornings as I waited to buy the weekend meat,
It will make a man of you.

Then he would show me round to the back
where the sides of cows hung from hooks
flesh blood dripping on to sawdust.

Go on, he insisted, get stuck in,
and I would punch the carcass
until my knuckles split and became bloody –

beyond the pain, I was ecstatic,
Soften it up, he urged, soften it up.

My father would never let me do boxing
years later I understood:
when I think of the thud of fist on flesh
I remember how he softened them up first
before abusing them.

Gypsy Ballads

This is my death
the thud of iron rings on the seawall
at the harbour
corks on water
and if the Spanish waitresses smile
tell me this old man blind in his eyes
knew Lorca on the high Sierra
I know they are lying
I know the wind in the olive groves
I know the taste of a shared cigarette
that castles flaming in the sky
are storytelling
and this is not the Galician coast
where all those years ago
you stood on the balcony of a fleapit hotel
and bared all to the children begging in the square
a laughing girl drunk on sun and cheap brandy
running with the bulls of literature
through a Spain not yet overrun:
we are closer to nine glens
a water dark from the sea loughs
I see myself dying in you
the memories dimming
flying away like Sunday's chip-papers
closing down like the old penny arcades and circuses
where each morning now
is a basin of waste covered over with a towel,
Will you eat something today?
A slice of dry toast?
A biscuit?
This is what is left to us
the soiled wads of cotton
the harried nurses who are polite
but not of our generation
the dog-eared college book
the misunderstanding of words read through mist.

Christine McNeill

Crossword

Our heads bent to the clue:
Danish composer.
Your searching thoughts

a ladder for mine to climb –
one rung higher to guess the first syllable –
I could die to find the word.

When it strikes,
the other catches it
and in unison we blurt it out –

quick-lightning speed,
collaborative:
such closeness is rarely achieved.

Later,
sitting without words
deep in a place below

our moody interior
where silence
is like infinity's glass door,

I recall how
we connected
while doing the crossword

and ponder on the idea of love:
you smile at me, with my unkempt hair,
and I at you, unshaven:

we sit, waiting for further clues.
You say: *It's nothing to do with ideas –
it's something that comes from the heart.*

Jean O'Brien

Blue Bobbin

Its dull case an ornament
in the corner, its use almost
forgotten. someone has taken
the table of the Singer sewing
machine, once everyone had one.
If you lifted it out you could turn
the handle instead of footing
the treadle. Gone, along
with the table is the drawer
that held bobbins, my delight,
as a child sifting the
spools of rainbow thread.

When my mother sewed
she favoured the blue bobbin.
All our curtains, whatever the colour,
were backed with blue stitches.
I helped her thread the needle
through a maze of eyes and hooks
down to where the thread vanished
into a small silver box.
Like a magician pulling an endless
stream of hankies from his sleeve;
it conjured another thread
and together, they and we,
formed the stitch.

At night when mother was busy
I used to slide the lid on the silver
chamber to see if I could figure out its trick.
I only saw the small half-moon lever
moving back and over
and like a hidden slice of sky,
the edge of a blue bobbin peeping out.

Julie-ann Rowell

Lightning

You called to say only two people so far
had died by lightning, on motorbikes,
while you travelled home in a car's luxury.

You said the rain came down like iron, a trick
to turn homes into graves, thunder like artillery –
the monsoon, yet they prayed and longed for it.

I'm home by the window on the garden
watching house sparrows in the lantern tree
in the mildest of breezes, a snuffle in the leaves.

Only *two* today you said, in this country where
there's a god for everything, the sun has a face,
the lightning many names, and reasons.

A strike once hollowed and blackened the trunk
of a chestnut tree in the woods beyond our garden.
The ribbon of wind beyond the glass cannot reach me.

Jet-Lag

I've a mouth full of bees when I disembark,
a different country and it's never easy
crossing borders, especially with you out there

beyond the railing with expectant face,
like first love, when you can't let go
and any hurdle's worth the trouble.

So here I am with a sting on my lips,
bruised with people, lugging the heaviest case
in history, past the chauffeurs,

wanting the happy beginning, yet it's like
I'm learning to walk; I slept my way
into the new world – in my brain, it's the middle

of the night, and I instinctively reject the glaring
light as I keep myself up. It's hopeless,
I'm all thumbs and mood, but you still believe

with your hands reaching out to me. Together
we will stretch time to fit, and perhaps
I'll open my mouth and find honey.

Fiona Sampson

Angels of the Coffee Shop

In the coffee shop
you explain orthodoxy.
World is fallen light.

Then you must be angels,
the light from the window behind you
snagging the anorak

on the back of each chair,
catching your hair
ruffled-up by March wind,

is no accident
when it falls pane by pane
on the ordinary pine

of your table.
Shy angels
with carrier bags, who know bliss

is in and beyond
this crowded café, pray for me
while hands or spoons

brighten in turn –
here and there they
touch the room to rapture.

Belinda Cooke

Salt Water

Tide holds the summer voices,
salt sticks to my chapped fingers,
curve of outgoing surf, magnified leaves:
Inverewe's cacophonous avenue of trees.

Here for our separate reasons
it's as if we are looking
into each other's bones –
me trying to get to where you are.

Water, summer green, masks its
olive dark connection with the wind
I watch you as you set off uphill
after lost views in the camera's lens…

I cannot feel these shadows
crossing *Coigach* the way you do,
perfection a flaw we cannot fathom –
like surf on the beach, I know.

Sue Roe

Piano d'Enfant

a stick and bells
hair like strands of silk at the neck
meeting place between stem and leaf

and the merry-go-round's still creaking
the rag book's ancient songs
douce for the doll's house dolls

the child asleep
meeting place between stem and leaf,
stem, the rag book's songs

Psyche

first irises of spring
a boy on the staircase with flowers
each a smeared mouth

a purple sound
winged like a thing unseen
scented with wood notes

sometimes the sky is torn
scarlet comes threaded through grey
uncanny as woodwind

he closes the door
I climb the stairs to my room
thinking of oboes, irises

their yellow tongues hanging out
they are flinging their violet heads back

June Hall

Weeping Woman

(Thoughts of Picasso and Dora Maar as they observe his portrait of her)

He dislocates my face with sorrow,
  deconstructs my mouth, chills it blue,
plunders the black and white of me;
    needs me to weep, roar, fragment
      so he can dissect
    and butcher me like scrag end of mutton;

    I paint her flaunting velvet hat, tilt it into madness,
    slice the many-coloured pieces of clown-mask from her face
        to show on canvas flesh scraped bare -

    He displaces my eyes, crossing them with unshed tears,
  twists the cheerful red and yellow of my hat,
then with loaded brush stabs a blaze of blue on its brim.
  He paints me in blood and acid (a footnote
      to the larger tableau of war), signs the canvas
  with a flourish, a warrant for my slaughter

          I fragment her bones, sections of white finger clutching
          jags of grief; I dissect her screams in vomit-blue
                and splinter her teeth to sharpen the bite

(Picasso painted *Weeping Woman* in 1937, the same year he finished *Guernica*)

Felix Dennis

My Generation

I thought that I might be the first to fall,
    But not at all;
I buried them with saplings at their head –
    The cold, the dead.
The lonelier I grew, the more I sought
    (Yet never caught)
The murmuring of souls upon the wing.
    No bell would ring
For those who once had rallied to my side –
    To kiss, to chide.
Now I am as you see me, and alone;
    An autumn drone
Outside a failing hive of paper vaults.
    And yet, our faults
Were less than had we replicated chance –
    We danced the dance
Because we never knew the world was flat.
    We danced! Say that!

The Big 'A'

'We think we have brains, but the truth is brains have us'.
Andrea Gillies: *Keeper: Living with Nancy. A Journey in Alzheimers*

Of where I squat – I know not what,
Nor how, nor when or why,
And yet I know... that long ago
This wasteland was not I.

No friendly star shows where we are
Or how we came to this.
My mind has left to scout a cleft
That leads to the abyss.

And though I yearn for its return
It wanders where it will.
A month? A day? – I cannot say,
Its voices haunt me still.

We think we have brains – a key
Philosophers discuss,
And yet they make a grave mistake:
Our brains, instead, have us.

Tony Roberts

Drawndark

You are in and out of the room
undressing, night dressing, a toothbrush
in your mouth. The light is silvered.
You pause a moment – no toothbrush now –
and ask, *Have you stopped reading, love?*
Yes I have stopped, puzzled at the word
smokefall – and then to watch you
as you move about the room.
I still adore this privacy
of seeing you in silhouette,
the dark repetition of these
nightly little ceremonies
calling forth new coinages: *smokefall,*
drawndark, my heart a moonlit book.

Houses at Naples, 1782

for Charles Tomlinson

Through an oil sketch on paper
of crumbling masonry walls
pitted with scaffolding holes
we enter the silent kingdom
our notions of the past
worn as this washing slumped
in the windows of a still day.

Jorge Luis Borges

1964

*Translated from the Spanish by **Terese Coe***

i

Already the world has no magic. They have
left you. You will not be sharing the clear moon
again, nor the slow-paced gardens. Already
there is no moon that is not a mirror of

the past, a prism of solitude, a sun
of pain and grief. Goodbye to the joined
hands and the temples that moved toward love.
Today you have only your faithful memory

and your days that are a desert. No one loses
anything (you say once more in vain)
except what he does not have and has never

had, but it's not enough to be brave
to learn the art of forgetting. A symbol, a rose,
can tear you apart. A guitar can slaughter you.

ii

I will never be happy again. Maybe
it doesn't matter. There are so many other
things in the world; any moment whatever
is deeper and more various than the sea.

Life is short and though the hours are so long,
a shadowy strangeness observes us,
death, that other ocean, that other arrow
that frees us from the sun and the moon

and from love. The happiness you gave me
and took away must be undone;
what once was everything will have to be nothing.

All I have left is the pleasure in being
sad. That useless quirk that turns me
to the South, to a certain door, to a certain corner.

John Gladwell

No Cure Yet

From this field of names, take one,
Write it down until it belongs to you,
Reshape each story, give it a different ending,
New characters, a new location,

With nothing now left to belong to except
This corridor of trees, this crematorium,
Stopping the car to allow a cortège to pull past,
MUM spelt out in flowers, as you then squeeze my hand,

Eyes closed, watching the sky ache
And listening to your breathing,
As quiet as thought, where all the poems
And all the Holy Books are now their own disease,

No cure yet and in the distance, dice rattling,
As the clock waits, counting itself backwards
Then counting itself out of time, a theory of chaos,
A theory of everything these shadows can no longer contain.

Rosie Shepperd

I want to think you'll make a neat job of confiscating my heart

It's up to you, but here's an idea.
$$It could be not dissimilar$$
to the removal of Anne Boleyn's head.
I read that when he saw the neatness of her muslin cap,
and the whiteness of her neck,
the executioner hesitated, called
fetch my sword to distract them both.
He dismissed her
before she could gather
anything.

I feel foolish but I am not unwise.
Your perception of pain is not unlike
garden furniture
left out past September.
It assumes infinite tolerance to seasons;
little understanding of temperature,
the reversible effects of corrosion,
the garrulous nature of slugs.
I know your concentration will be
dipping now,
so before you start, I promise:
There will be no untidiness and it will make
almost no noise.

Patricia McCarthy

A Little Big Book

Tim Liardet: *Priest Skear*, Shoestring Press, 2010

Poets from time immemorial have been inspired to write about the sea which does, after all, occupy four-fifths of the earth's surface. From the anonymous poet of *The Seafarer* to Whitman, Emily Dickinson, Anne Bronte, Hart Crane, Wallace Stevens and Robert Frost (as presented in an inspiring anthology of poems on the sea, *The Sea! The Sea!*, edited by Peter Jay, Anvil Press, 2005), the sea exerts its fascination in all its different facets: as a powerful, exhilarating, beautiful, life-giving force, as warlike and protective but also as a deadly hostile killer.

Though presented in a modest pamphlet, Tim Liardet's sequence, *Priest Skear*, is a memorable masterpiece. It is not merely a 'sea poem' about a threatening, destructive sea, but a powerful political allegory about our whole society, offering a critique of justice/injustice, blame, of prejudice, racism, and of immigration policies themselves. Seamus Heaney once said in an interview that politics should only be tackled 'at an angle' in poetry; otherwise the poem becomes a mere slogan. It is this 'angle', rather than head-on confrontation, that Liardet succeeds in managing so articulately.

Concentrating on the drowning of twenty three vulnerable, exploited Chinese cocklepickers in Morecambe Bay which hit the news in 2004, this collection shows the plight of illegal immigrants who work as slaves of debt bondage, exploited by gangmasters. It is a timely microcosm of the imperfections in the system of the 'Albion' that we live in today where migrant workers, even if illegal, need more protection, understanding and compassion.

While not actually a shipwreck – though the Priest Skear rock resembled the hull of a boat before it sank – the 'Priest Skear' sequence links to Hopkins' 'The Wreck of the Deutschland' in its large canvas, and in its dealing with a tragedy which is a public event. Liardet's critique of today's society is subtly and cleverly embedded in his text, in its tone and imagery so that the reader has to be active in teasing out its full impact. Hopkins' more overt 'Wreck of the Deutschland', by contrast, which entailed the latter's conversion to Catholicism, was a Christian allegory, the drowned souls chosen to go up to God, their maker. Liardet's treatment of the Chinese cocklepickers' plight off the English coast, in contrast, highlights the terrible futility of the accident, its waste, as well as the injustice and prejudice involved, despite the present so-called tolerant, multi-cultural society.

Liardet's poems are honed, incisive, not a word too many, not a word out of place. His startlingly accurate, resonant imagery, his focus on random objects that gain a special poignancy, his use of body parts that even become part of the sea – 'their clavicles rock-pools, their breast-points twirled weed' and of metonymy, with a group of people representing a single body, as in an earlier collection, *The Blood Choir*, give this book its multi-layered delivery. Technically too, it is masterfully achieved with its clever patterns and forms. 'Priest Skear', the sequence of twelve finely-accomplished, harrowing poems in couplets, is the nugget at the centre of the book, with interlinking poems serving as bookends, before and after. This gives the collection a somewhat disturbing symmetry. What's more, Liardet proves himself to be as musically adept a handler of the different uses of repetition for effect both within individual poems and woven throughout the poems, as TS Eliot in *Four Quartets* as he reiterates motifs, leit-motifs, resonances, crescendos, and codas. Indeed, the chains of repetition resemble the water gushing, gurgling and swirling into everywhere, including into the reader for total immersion, evoking a helpless feeling of no escape.

The introductory poem, a portrait of a Chinese man in 'Chinaman Shy' sets the ironical tone of the political allegory that this little big book is. The clever metaphor of the 'Shy', like a coconut shy usually used for fun, familiar to all, is sustained sinisterly through the poem. Liardet suggests that the figure of the Chinaman smiling through all the odds has persisted through centuries with a peculiar resilience: 'Every time you are pinged down'... 'a head grows back to replace the one blown away'. He even 'pops up' in our unconscious, 'slither-limbed'. The line 'you Chinese are so many, so many' is the poet parodying the comments of intolerant compatriots who refuse to see a foreign nation, particularly one they do not like, as consisting of individuals, each important to someone. The poem resolves in the poet's sympathetic but unsentimentalised view of 'the poor'...'always there to be sacrificed' – in this case the illegal immigrants who 'crowd for a cheap passage whatever the risk'. This poem is followed by two further, different introductory poems addressed to the poet's father that show Liardet's personal ability to identify with the cocklepickers and to mirror them movingly. The poet remembers his near drowning at the age of four, the 'pedals of his feet' riding 'the ghostly velocipede' as he sank, almost strangled by weed 'until you fished me out like a pup from the drowning bucket'. The second poem, 'The Interment', beautifully describes the aftermath of his father's saving him from drowning. The little boy/poet, while craving a return into 'the glimmering' sea that had taught him 'the vitality of fear which felt like reverence', innocently buries his father, apart from his head, 'in a dolmen of wet sand'. Several of the doomed Chinese cocklepickers were later found buried likewise in the sand, with only the head showing after what Liardet – seemingly lightheartedly but with seriously destructive undertones – defines as 'the sea's play'.

Similarly, after the end of the 'Priest Skear' sequence, come the poet's conclusions, again from different perspectives, on the event. The wonderfully strong coda, 'Stigmata', with the ironic Christian associations in its heading, questions the justice of laying all the blame for the tragedy on the gangmaster, Lin Liang Ren and sentencing him to fourteen years in prison for his part in the drownings and for manslaughter. Clothes are used as elsewhere, this time internalised metaphorically: the blame 'passes through the weft of your overcoat and vest/ and finds only these bone buttons, dark inside your skin.' The rhythmical patter of 'And the salt-mark of the sea has reached your waist' repeated with his 'chest' and 'chin' is like a rant in anger at the injustice of making a scapegoat of this man only, when facts get blurred and the implication is that not only other gangmasters, but our very immigration policies and prejudiced attitudes should also take the blame. The 'ducking' of his 'childish cheek' hints at his innocence, though 'When the Atlantic thunders, it thunders through you, / while your pilot flame is tearing, tearing at its wick', yet he is unable to re-light 'one last match'.

'The Living and the Drowned', another end poem, takes a fresh view of the tragedy by highlighting those 'sneaked-in Chinese' who, by fluke, escaped the drowning simply because 'the boneshaker' of a van they were in broke down. 'The Ghost of the Chinese Laundry on Threadneedle Street' links back not only to one of the introductory poems, 'Riding the Ghostly Velocipede', but also to the previous poem where in the aftermath of 'what might have happened', the future would be 'inspecting' the ghosts' of those who missed the cocklepicking. This is a particularly poignant poem describing a certain Yick Wo who works day in day out on his semi-outdated worn-out press whose lid's 'mouth-hinge emits a sort of stifled wail,/ as if trying to remember some great symphony/ its squeak is merely a stray snivel of'. This steam-press is further personified; it is 'Like an old toothless monster done with marauding'. The last stanza is a clever indictment of our patriarchal, racially-prejudiced system. The poet gives a set of rules or advice on enduring stoically whatever bad treatment is meted out in the heartless voice of, perhaps, some government or immigration official. The tone is redolent of Confucian philosophy endorsing the work ethic, but the words are damning to their core. The last line: 'You do our dirty work and we'll never forgive you' in the vernacular of those in power is a wry comment on the unjust treatment of migrants, illegal or not.

The penultimate end-poem of the book, in which the poet observes 'every final word' is 'mimed with no sound at all', is a very moving poem for Gua Binlong. This victim was recorded in the national press as making a last call to his wife 5,000 miles away while the water was rising – Liardet graphically imagines it – from his 'knees', 'thighs', to his 'waist', 'sternum', 'mouth' 'as he yelled into the mouthpiece/ of his state-of-the-art, touchscreen phone'.

The very last poem of the book, 'The Gap between the Boards of the Pier', links back to the two poems the poet/child addresses to his father in the introductory session to the collection, completing the wonderfully-constructed pattern of the whole. Here is another childhood memory framing 'Priest Skear', illustrating how profound an impression the Atlantic made on the boy as he peered through the planks – 'it sucked you in and out, you thought, grew dark'. This both foretold what would happen years later to the Chinese cocklepickers and prompted the poet's inspiration for this book. Even back then, 'it brought close to you the terrible presence of *depth*'.

'Depth' is what the central 'Priest Skear' sequence is all about. The imagery is so powerful, so interwoven that the reader lives through the cocklepickers' drowning as if it is happening to him/her. 'Priest Skear' astounds with its athletic verbal virtuosity, coupled with alliterative gymnastic movements recalling Gerard Manley Hopkins, and up/down Miltonic fluctuations for effect; in Liardet's case these are closely tied in with the cohesion of the sequence, and its mathematical precision. The clever juxtaposition of 'They go down' in the first line of poems 1-3 is followed by 'They come up' in the first line of poems 4-6, followed by the remaining 6 poems starting alternately with 'They go down' and 'They come up' which does several things. It subtly questions the accuracy of media coverage (i.e. what is really happening?); it dramatically speeds up the event, and, in terms of imagery, links back to the very first poem, 'Chinaman Shy' where 'Every time you are pinged down, shouts one/ the metal plate hoists you back into place'. The sea with its 'tonnage' and 'volume' is personified as the threatening 'maker and disguiser of powers'; it has its own 'physics'. Numbers are important throughout and give the sequence its realism, magnifying the horror, and increasing the desperation. For example, groups of words appear in threes such as 'goodbye, goodbye, goodbye', 'go down, go down,/ go down'. There is no 'tapped watch' to tell them 'to turn back./ turn back, turn back'. Numbers are also used as subtraction: 'as Priest Skear's last sinking metre of crag/ sinks to fifty, to thirty, to twenty centimetres,// to two, to one, and is gone'. 'The ghosts/ of forty hands' reach out for the helicopter's ladder. They resemble a single 'great straining net of herring'. (In Hopkins, to God the Father 'the goal was a shoal' of souls). The number one is particularly relevant as the drowning group are peculiarly 'bound to each other' 'like a system of branches'. They go down 'with one snarl. One snarl. One throat'. When they surface, they cling 'like a sail – a raft of survivors'. Here they are depersonalised to become 'it': 'It can cling. It can swim'. This 'it' satirically predicts and mimics the prejudiced language used by the arrogant Englishman in the next few lines of direct speech. Hearing that some of the Chinese are safe, he comes out with: 'what a shame, what a shame, he says,/ *these little fuckers got so good at swimming'*.

The use of the lyrical for the hideous is an ingenious device for highlighting horror. Liardet's 'sea rose// of a haemorrhage worn in the left ear', and the clothes ripped off by the drowning in the fight for their lives which are 'like bright sea flowers, like Mayday signals' demonstrate this only too well. So also do the random objects he picks out and anchors to the situation by tying them to place-names on this hazardous coast – such as the 'drenched gilet hung/ by its arm-hole from Hollow Scar' and the 'yellow pantaloons, legs apart, hooked/ around the pelvis of Haws Point'. In a way, too, the oblivious playing of the brass band in a local pub near to the disaster is an example of what seems on the surface lyrical, but is the opposite. This satirical use of musical 'play', that Alexander Pope would have been proud of, in the penultimate poem in the 'Priest Skear' sequence, not only brings to a crescendo the other forms of 'play' already noted but also accentuates the poet's horror at these oblivious musicians – the men who should have warned the cocklepickers about the dangers of the gale force six and the tide – practising on their cornets and different kinds of horns, 'the four-valve Euphonium the pulling power'. Here the down/up movements reach their crescendo along with the band: 'As the Chinese go down, the band goes trembling up/ and trembles, trembles to crescendo... building around the deep voice// of the trombone pumping out like a hearbeat/ the bottommost bass line of *The Keel Row'*. Liardet's choice of *The Keel Row*, an English north-eastern folk song about a boat, the *keel*, carrying a young lad whose beloved lass wishes for his safety is charming and light and suits the cold-blooded locals who play its melody, but throws into dramatic contrast the real heavy songless drama being played out in the sea outside. The alliteration of the heavy 'b' here booms out its cruel irony as if from the bottom of the sea where the Chinese victims have no 'heartbeat' at all.

Language is a theme, considering the tragedy was in part brought on by the language barrier the Chinese were experiencing: 'the words on warning-boards, say their eyes,/ were written in a language we did not speak'. Liardet handles this brilliantly. ' A few of the rescued 'chatter out in mime the best of Babel's gibberish' according to the barbaric English rescuers that the poet mocks for seeing the migrants as 'an embarrassment (new collective noun) of Chinese' and for claiming heartlessly 'Drowned men are never drowned enough', especially when the survivors 'are here for good'. As the rest drown, they are either reduced to a dumb language: 'Find us/ the culpable, say their mouths full of darkness'. 'Hack off the gangmaster's head – say their hands'... but 'If one gang opens up/ another opens up behind it, another behind that'... 'We lived in hovels, say their stony eyes, and now our tongues/ are frozen forever in a furrow of ice.' Or 'the words they'll never speak/ and which will never enter history, never be heard// and never recorded' go down with them. 'The Atlantic swallows the lot', gagging them: all the semantics, linguistic history of 'the fifty thousand characters/ currently fattening in the Kangxi dictionary or perched// on the tongue of Mandarin Pinyin'. Also going down with them, surrealistically, into the vortex is what their lives consist of: their extended families, and possessions, all numbered, including the not yet paid for 'two hundred items of discount furniture' and their debts: 'eleven crates of unpaid, final reminders', including fun, probably cheap, tacky possessions linking back to the coconut shy image in the very first poem: 'eight pop-pop bikes', 'two battered pedal cars' (harking back to the early poem about the ghostly velocipede), and 'One parrot named Tsu-Li'. By listing their possessions and their relations, the poet builds up a picture of their normal lives in China, eliciting our sympathy for them and making them flesh and blood individuals, not just 'migrants'.

In a general way, the allegory that this collection is can be stretched wider, beyond the circumstances of the particular disaster described, with all its concomitant concerns. The sea can be seen to represent, in Jungian terms, the unconscious in which we are all at risk of drowning, in which all our identities are questioned, and in which we all struggle to survive as well as to articulate ourselves in the most communicable language possible, while clinging to other humans in the inescapable face of death. Liardet hints at this level and layer with extreme subtlety, slipping into his text almost unnoticeable allegorical figures without their customary initial capital letter. The poet/boy in one of the first poems learnt 'the vitality of fear which felt like reverence', this fear or *angst* being a condition in which most of us live existentially, alongside 'the monster of survival' that we struggle to hang on to. The 'neglect' defined by the poet is what in our society we are guilty of; it was 'neglect, like a shifty old ghost, turned to stones/ that were tied to their ankles and wrists' that caused the Chinese cockle-pickers' tragedy in the first place and will cause others like it. Even if reprieved by 'reverence', we are all, in the biggest sense, in 'the fellowship of the drowned'.

David Cooke

All that Absence Signifies

Ian Parks: *The Landing Stage,* Lapwing, Belfast, 2010

Following closely on the heels of *Love Poems 1979-2009* (Flux Gallery Press, 2009) and two exquisite recent collections, *Shell Island* (The Waywiser Press, 2006) and *The Cage* (Flux Gallery Press, 2008), *The Landing Stage* is further testimony to the gifts of a poet who for three decades has gone his own way, unmoved by fashion or hype, and whose talent is still far from receiving its due. Quintessentially, Parks has always been a lyric poet whose work is characterized by its surefooted technique, its musicality, and its uniquely elegiac cadences. However, in *The Landing Stage* we see him pushing beyond his normal boundaries as he also finds a place for two highly ambitious, extended works: his enigmatic, Chandleresque narrative, *Noir,* and *The Double Man,* a sustained meditation upon the life and work of W. H. Auden, who has long been Parks' acknowledged master.

The collection opens with 'The Northern Lights', an edgy, existential piece which sets the tone for the collection as a whole and whose protagonist is an outsider, a loner, perhaps, and an observer of others' lives:

> The doorstep is the perfect place to be:
> from its bright corner you can hear
>
> the sound of neighbours coming home
> and from its recess you can see
> the black antennae sharp against the sky.

He is also a seeker of meanings, however illusory this search may be: 'Looking but not knowing / what it is I'm looking for // I step back from the shadows, / pass unseen into the house...' A similar sense of separation also informs 'The Girl In The Garden' which describes the bedraggled figure of a girl or a young woman who, in spite of all entreaties, refuses to come in from the rain because 'What she was is everything / while what she might be matters less and less.' In 'Sleeping On The Island' the poet sees again through adult eyes the lonely figure of a beachcomber he envied as a child, but whose existence he now sees in a different light, knowing that 'solitude is often love denied'. Like the great Italian poet Eugenio Montale whose stoic lyricism is not dissimilar to his own, Parks has frequently been drawn to shorelines and sea views and nowhere more impressively than in the superbly poised 'Beach Fire':

> A fire is burning somewhere. At midnight
> on this stretch of empty shore.
> I see a red glow pulsing through the dunes
> and know that someone out there
> took the time to scoop a hollow
> in the sand, line the rim with stones
> then gather driftwood from the beach
> to light it, feed it, keep its heart alive.
>
> I know more of them than they of me
> but know them only through the dying flame;
> the smoke that drifts across to sting my eyes.
> Like me, they must have thought they were alone
> Which in itself invites complicity.
> For both of us there's stillness, darkness, doubt;
> perception shutting out what's on the edge
> of a cold sea ruled by a cold moon.

Much of Parks' previous work, and in particular his love poems, has taken the form of brief, concentrated narratives in which atmosphere is built up cinematically as the poet homes in on details. This technique is taken to a further level in *Noir*, a suspenseful narrative extending over four pages, in which ambiance is all and plot details are merely hinted at. It depicts an uneasy world of glistening streets, bleary lights and waterfront hotels, where 'The desk clerk reads philosophy... / is distant and obsessed // by the problem of evil / and the fact of other minds.' It's across this cityscape that a man and a woman seem to be moving towards an encounter, although the precise nature of their relationship is never made entirely clear. The second of the two lengthier pieces, *The Double Man*, consists of two sections divided respectively into eighteen and fifteen quatrains, evoking the duality of W. H. Auden, the archetypal Englishman and hero of the left in the Thirties who went on to become an American citizen and a convert to Kierkegaardian Christianity. A Dantesque encounter in which Parks follows in the footsteps of Eliot and Heaney, the poem starts by conjuring up the presence of the master:

                                                I knew
him by the way he cupped his hand
around the sharp-drawn instant
of a cigarette to be the spokesman
of the border and the group, boyish
in this drab, ill-fitting suit, who flicked
his Thirties crop back from his eyes...

It then moves on to describe that derelict, post-industrial landscape so
familiar from Auden's early work, but which also forms a part of Parks' own
Yorkshire mining inheritance. The poem concludes with Auden exhorting his
acolyte to be true to himself, and to accept that: 'What it comes down to in
the end / is the love of a handful of people.'

Other poems in which Parks beautifully distils the influence of Auden are
'The Last Boat Leaving', a variation on the 'quest' theme, and 'Rain On A
Summerhouse Roof':

No news is made today:
no armies mobilise on dark frontiers,
no landslides, earthquakes, tidal waves
to take the headlines by surprise ...

There will be no announcements from the state.
Only the rain on a summerhouse roof
and this wet August morning waking me
to the last of England petering out...

Although he has now turned fifty, Parks had only published one full-length
collection before the appearance of *Shell Island* in 2006, yet what is so
impressive, given the proliferation of his recent offerings, is how consistently
excellent they are. Like its predecessors, *The Landing Stage* is full of poems
which, whilst seeming at first understated and almost self-effacing, manage by
virtue of their musical resonance, their attention to detail, and the timelessness
of their inspiration, to draw one in and alter one's perceptions of reality. Parks,
it seems, has an unfailing ability to evoke the presence of an object and then,
effortlessly, to transcend it in poems such as 'Paper Lanterns', which make
'known darkness / suddenly more strange', or 'Screen', where a trellis screen in
a bedroom seems 'an illusion' that 'shows more than it hides', whilst 'Feathers'
is imbued with hints of otherworldliness, 'the sense of something // having
come and gone, / something lost and never found.' This is a feeling which is
again captured in the wonderful closing lines of the collection's title poem:

From the deck the landscape has
a different kind of look:
flatter, thinner, limitless.

I'm in no rush to get across
though everyone I've ever loved
is waving from the other side.

At a time when so much contemporary 'poetry' seems complacently mired in the mundane, Parks is a poet to buy and to keep. Embodying the classical virtues of truth and focus, his burnished lines are impressive, memorable and deeply felt. Both scrupulous and inspired, he is a poet who respects language and for whom we should be grateful.

Alex Smith

Of Form and Narrative

Eiléan Ní Chuilleanáin: *The Sun-Fish,* The Gallery Press
Fiona Sampson: *Rough Music,* Carcanet Press, 2010
Jo Shapcott: *Of Mutability,* Faber, 2010
Linda Saunders: *The Watchers,* Arrowhead Press, 2009
Linda France: *You are Her,* Arc, 2010

Eiléan Ní Chuilleanáin's recent volume of poems, *The Sun-Fish*, has won the prestigious International Griffin Poetry Prize for 2010. According to my reckoning this is her eighth collection of poems but for those who are unfamiliar with her work, *The Sun-Fish* is a good place to start.

Ní Chuilleanáin is clearly an exponent of the principle that the unit of a poem is the line but her poems are more than demonstrative in this respect; they have a carved, lapidary feel to them, as though chiselled into the page. A second characteristic is that her poems appear to be narratives, powerfully voiced in their act of telling. With only a few exceptions, almost any poem you turn to in the Faber/Gallery *Selected* begins as though at the start of a story: 'When all this is over, said the swineherd ...' ('Swineherd'), 'I sent the girl to the well ...' ('The Water Journey'). It is this aspect, however, which is deceptive; a large number of Ní Chuilleanáin's poems *read* as straightforward narratives when they are not, or not that simply, in the sense that they lead the reader along a linear storyline through to a conclusion. In so many poems the lines enounce the progress of an apparent story with a confident ring, only to engage with ambiguity and enigma:

> She opens the stopcock and lets it come bubbling up
> Filling as far as the reinforced glass floor
> And it shines transparent ...
>
> She gazes in the deep tank, picks out
> The shadows meeting, herself;

which leads finally to:

> So, was it her arm that sliced
> Half a gown away, the silver

Fall, her hand that cut the last line from the letter,
That laid the rooms all open, with their cramped air,
Their claw-footed cooking stoves
And their turned-down beds?

('The Savage')

Though apparently clear at first, the poem becomes increasingly enigmatic.
In 'After Drinking the Dragon's Blood' we have:

The pigeon as big as a dog
Explains in his shambling grammar:
All this tuning holds back meaning
While setting it free.

This comes close to Marianne Moore's 'Poetry' – there are things important
'beyond all this fiddle' and Ní Chuilleanáin is saying something similar: 'All
this tuning holds back meaning / while setting [the poem] free.' It would be
unhelpful to start discussing what 'the poems are about' because that can very
quickly lead to 'what a poem says' and, in that respect, it is worth recalling
the wise words of I A Richards, that a poem is not what it says but what it
is. I believe that much of Ní Chuilleanáin's poetry is rooted in origins, or
the symbols of origins, how they infuse and connect to the reader's interior
landscapes: blood, hair, eggs:

When she opened the egg the wise woman had given her,
she found inside some of her own hair and a tooth, still
bloody, from her own mouth.

(from *The Rose-Geranium*, 1981)

and

The soaking tears of centuries drill down
Low passages in between the stones,
Keeping to the calendar made out

In columns of names, a single stiff skin
Coiled up and stowed away in the high slit
Above the stone corbel that once had human features.

('The Litany')

One could have expected this poem, included in the present collection, to have ended here, but it concludes ambiguously with: 'The wave can pause no longer, called back to Brazil' on a separate line to itself. Is this the unceasing Heraclitean flux where stone corbels 'once had human features' and the waves of time, no less than vast oceans, lap on human shores, Brazil standing for anywhere, distant and out of reach?

And there are the many bridges and directions that occur throughout the poetry, which both factually and metaphorically are so much a part of our early lives. It is this *pressure* of origins, both atavistic and from childhood, that so often impinges on the poems. 'The Cold' seeks to express this:

> ... I search for a known phrase:

> Only four friendly words open their locks, and those
> Are stuck like treasures in the grip of grammar, morose,
> giving nothing away. *Memory*, and then *Alone*,

> *Memorial*, and *Creation*. I am alone here, I can stay
> As long as I please in the cold, printing images in my brain.

This poem is at the heart of *The Sun-Fish* with its searching for profound but personal roots in our language. This brings us inevitably to myth; if Ní Chuilleanáin's narratives are deceptive and enigmatic, then they have the power of myth:

> *Stop*, said the angel. *Stop* doing what you were doing and listen ...

> I am the angel who says *Remember*,
> Do you remember, the taste of the wood-sorrel leaves
> In the ditches on your way to the school? Go on,
> Remember, how you found them
> Piercing a lattice of green blades,
> And their bitter juice.

> ('Michael and the Angel')

and:

> Do you remember the dark night
> When the voice cried from the yard
> Asking for water, and you rose from the bed.
> You were gone so long, I said to myself at last
> *As long as I live I will never ask who was there*.

('In the Mountains')

Memory, clouded with mystery, becomes myth, giving expression to who we are in the here and now. We remember the dark night and a voice crying (in the yard, the garden or the next room) but we will never know who was there; the experience becomes a part of our personal mythology, always ready to take us again by surprise, in shock.

*

After Fiona Sampson's previous volume of poems, *Common Prayer* (Carcanet, 2007), with its extraordinary fusing of the numinous, the erotic and close – but never exploitative – study of suffering, readers will have eagerly awaited the book that follows, *Rough Music*. They will not be disappointed. Although similar techniques are employed – the playing with form, the free verse which, when looked at closely, is not *that* free when the organic structures and control of the poems are considered – *Rough Music* takes quite a different direction. For all its variation of textures, we are never far from suffering in *Common Prayer*, with its haunting 'Scenes from the Miracle Cabinet', Sampson's own 'metaphysic of presence' which moves to the wrenching rhythm of a hospital lift. But if *Common Prayer* offers variety and is not dominated by the bleakness of despair, then *Rough Music* too has many layers of meaning and sentiment at its core. *Rough Music*: in English folklore this is where a community visits humiliating punishment on those who have broken social taboos, as in Hardy's *The Mayor of Casterbridge*. The title poem, described as 'Songs without Tunes', leads us to a fresh narrative of Eurydice and Orpheus:

> Summer evenings at the weir:
> her body in green water
> or warm on the bank beside me
> as we shared a beer ...

says Orpheus, but Eurydice is

... the lost girl
a trace on the tape,
in the lens

That half-articulate blur ...

'Love is an eclipse' she cries,

I wanted to step into the light –
that vast silence

free of fists and hearts and rose tattoos,
flotsam and jetsam
of his need

'How could she just disappear?' wonders Orpheus and the reply he receives
from Hades is that they are all brought home, 'the bruised, the crushed, /
defaced, deflowered'; and so the love of the gentle Orpheus for Eurydice is
metamorphosed into the all-too-familiar story of vulnerable women mistreated
across the ages. Similarly with 'Charivari', the Continental equivalent of
rough music where loud and discordant crashing and banging of pots and
pans are made to serenade newlyweds, or as in the German *Katzenmusik*, an
intimidating, caterwauling row made to ridicule unequal marriages:

Fold the bed-sheet,
cross your fingers –
this lie you are
looks set to linger ...

like a rumour
or the smell
of last night's supper –
Wash the dishes,

cross your fingers ...

The sharp snare-drum rhythm employed here whips up the poem's momentum;
the female victim has nowhere to hide:

Difficult
to keep hidden,
bad blood leaks
around what's given –

Hell, or the *Inferno*, appears twice among the poems of *Rough* Music, and
with startling effect. The first instance has Dante in its title, '*Nel Mezzo*' from
the opening of the *Inferno*, but Sampson displaces that classic statement of
the mid-life crisis – lost in a gloomy wood without a path – with sparkling
wit right from the opening of the poem: ' ... and I find myself / in a garden / in
the lee of what must be / an ark', which is how it starts. The second instance,
however, is more sombre, in italics, and relates to Schubert's death:

the river's backdrop to the kiss
you borrowed from daylight
and bring to Dis

('Schubertiad')

Towards the end of the poem, Sampson says, without the slightest hint of
kitsch or sentimentality, 'You poor soul' and continues to the end in a moment
of near clairvoyance:

Without summer's garlands and girls
you're quite bare,
bespectacled, and alone
in that soiled bed.

There are not many poets who could get away with 'You poor soul' but
Sampson gives it the weight and gravity of meaning as if we are hearing it
(reading it) for the first time.

As in *Common Prayer*, Sampson takes time out, as it were, to contemplate
the inner, spiritual life. 'The Miracle Tree', a poem evoking the Saxon poem,
'The Dream of the Rood', begins:

The true Rood
is in the tree –

white
as rising sap,
the Christ-white blood

This is reminiscent of the spare, rigorous treatment found in the work of Pauline Stainer and, as with Stainer, there are no soft options, the matter of faith being gritty to the bone: 'The tree / holds up death - // ransacked body'. In 'Communion', Sampson employs the language of both communion and retreat:

> If I'm you, or you me –
> interpenetrating God –
> enlarge our intimacy

The tensions between identity and dwelling (indwelling) are skilfully articulated in 'At Käsmu', 'how to inhabit / (an identity, a place) fully,' what the French might call *bien dans sa peau*; although the poem is a self-conscious rumination, it avoids egotism:

> ... I drink my coffee and wonder
> how to phrase this problem,
> this matter of dwelling –
>
> or, more precisely, of not-dwelling.
> For what's in question is how to inhabit
> (an identity, a place) fully,
> which for Heidegger meant without reflection.
>
> ('At Käsmu')

Notwithstanding the rather jagged introduction of the prosaic 'Heidegger' into the line, we are brought in, *invited* into this process of meditation. 'At Käsmu' – discursive and thoughtful but not, in my view, at all rambling – is a key poem in this remarkable collection where the poet shifts between modes of consciousness and self-examination:

> Is this lying?
> (Here I interrupt myself
> to fiddle with the curtain.)
> Existentially, such a split is bad faith,
> but it's how we live –

This is a generous poetry where the self, far from seeking attention, is questioned closely but it is done with deftness of hand; *Rough Music* is a worthy successor to *Common Prayer* in every way.

*

Jo Shapcott's volume, *Of Mutability*, her first collection for twelve years, has been well received, and deservedly so. Here again we find an exuberant playing with form, despite the seriousness of underlying concerns. Many of the poems are ludic, inviting the reader to engage in the fun:

> Reader, you're an owl
> for this moment, your flower-
> face a white scrawl
> in the dark, a feather frill.
>
> ('Night Flight from Muncaster')

If these poems delight, then our delight is of the moment; we cannot escape from mutability, the rapid changes taking place in and around us all the time:

> Too many of the best cells in my body
> are itching, feeling jagged, turning raw ...

The volume starts with these opening lines from the sonnet, 'Of Mutability', with its dire *memento mori*:

> Look down these days to see your feet
> mistrust the pavement and your blood tests
> turn the doctor's expression grave.

Shapcott, having gone through a breast cancer experience, refuses to use the word; but if, in 'Procedure', the penultimate poem in the volume, she deals with it directly, there is no sense of self-pitying mawkishness:

> in my case, takes me back to the yellow time
> of trouble with blood tests, and cellular
> madness, and my presence required
>
> on the slab for the surgery ...

'My presence required' encapsulates the lightness of touch and wit that runs throughout this book, often reminiscent of the Metaphysical poets. Shelley's line, 'Nought may endure but Mutability', however, is exemplified in almost every poem, but if change is fleeting it can also be beautiful, bringing intense joy into our lives:

It's me, spinning inside
the brown foliage, laughing
and blink-squinting at every
here-gone, here-gone, here-gone
glimpse of the sun.

('Shrubbery')

The onset of the poet's aunt's dementia is handled with great tenderness and charm in 'Somewhat Unravelled':

She says ah ha! but I do
my crossword, don't I, OK not the difficult one, the one
with the wasname? Cryptic clues, Not that. I say,
auntie, little auntie, we were never cryptic ...

Language, inseparable from who we are, changes as we change. 'I appreciate your straight-on talk', says the poet to her aunt, 'the way you wish poetry / were just my hobby'.

Among the many satisfying variation of forms in this collection is the prose-poem, 'Scorpion', which deals with the killing of a scorpion with the heel of a shoe. 'I kill it because we cannot stay in the same room', it begins, and so on until it reaches its conclusion which is about the limitations of (non) language. So clear is its metaphoric reference – killing those that differ from us just because they *are* different – that if Shapcott had been a poet writing in the Eastern bloc during the Soviet era, 'Scorpion' would have got her into trouble. The poem reminded me of some of Zbigniew Herbert's miniature prose poems such as 'Wringer' and 'From the Technology of Tears' in this vein. In a further extension of the play of language there is an engaging mock Anglo Saxon riddle poem which ends with the poignant:

How
easily we part, adieu,
how often I leave trails
of myself in your wake.

Wit, as the Metaphysicals knew, comes from close observation as Shapcott illustrates; drowning in Earl Grey tea

127

                    might be a relief
          to drown that way and not

          in the fine wine he'd ploughed
          an expert front crawl through
          all these years.

                                        ('Tea Death')

Again, it is in the finely nuanced 'expert front crawl' that brings such poems
vividly to life. *Of Mutability* is a sparkling volume of poems, fresh and full
of energy, but whose polished surfaces should not be allowed to obscure the
seriousness that lies beneath.

                              *

The Watchers is Linda Saunders' second collection of poems. Her first, *Ways
of Returning*, was shortlisted for the Aldeburgh First Collection Prize in
2006. Many poems in *The Watchers* relate to how we grasp and hold things
in our vision as they pass. The book is divided into three sections which are
each prefaced with a quotation to this effect: Denise Levertov's 'Maybe what
seems evanescent is solid' starts the volume and helps to set the tone. Seeing
– grasping phenomena, especially natural forms, so that we give tangible
outline and structure to what is transient:

          Illusion of dolphins, backs arcing
          through a slipstream of light,
          beryl-blue water bounding ...

                                        ('Palimpsest')

   Sometimes, as in 'Playing Alone' (first published in *Agenda* Vol. 43 No.1),
the visual can be disconcerting if you are caught watching yourself: 'I'd turn
up the mirror on my mother's table', she says,

          always face down – to stop you falling
          in its echoing well, or cover a gaze
          that sees too much when you're not watching.

Both the examples of the dolphins and the child playing alone in the presence
of a mirror are expertly handled and serve to show how keenly observant
Saunders can be as a poet. However, there are times when Saunders can be
precious and over-explain when more should have been left to the reader. In

'The Dark Butterfly' for example she says:

> I always want to bring things into the light:
>> I set out little thoughts in dishes
>> to tempt them into the circle

For this reader the poet too often occupies an over-dominant role in a poem, telling the reader what is clearly implied anyway, which only leads to redundancies:

> His smile on my screen saver keeps beaming in
> above the Milky Way on that tee shirt
> I found at the Monterey Aquarium
> and brought back across 6000 miles
>
> of earth and ocean.

('Awesome')

I have quoted this at length because it illustrates what is perhaps too hasty an approach, leading to over-writing; across 6000 miles is acceptable but it is obvious that the journey is transcontinental, so why bring in 'of earth and ocean' which only serves to weaken the impact of the narrative? The poem itself is interesting in the way it marks out the poet's view of planets, 'the faint smudge of Sirtis Major', but I feel more could have been made of this aspect. In 'Luck', the poet, 'five months gone' takes a dramatic ride on a dirt road for twenty miles to a forest camp. She tucks her 'skirt close, edging past / poison oak, ants as long as my toenail', which again is sharply observed, but the poem as a whole suffers, is enervated by the prosaic: 'Nearby, prospectors had channelled a stream / down a wooden chute where they panned for gold'. The verse could easily have stopped at 'chute'; what else would prospectors be panning for in that place, and does it matter in the context of the poem? And we could have done without that 'nearby' which, as a connective, is too close to meanwhile back at the ranch.

   Linda Saunders' *The Watchers* is rather a mixed bag, therefore, with some closely and beautifully observed poems but the collection as a whole could have done with a little more editing, and with an eye kept out for those prosaic redundancies.

*

You are Her is Linda France's first collection since 2002, taking its title from a faded information board on Hadrian's Wall. Some of the poems deal with the riding accident the poet suffered in 1995 when she fractured her spine and cracked her pelvis. The injury re-emerged, the book cover informs us, 'in the form of flashbacks and chronic pain ten years later when several of her friends died in close succession'. However, instead of a series of poems offering a tightly focused and explicit narrative, the volume deals with this painful history only occasionally and usually obliquely. Terrible though the experience must have been, France does not button-hole the reader in self-pitying mode.

You are Her explores with vigour a variety of forms, and France is not afraid of some experimentation. The poem 'You Don't Know What Love Is', taken from the jazz standard, has every line of its couplets ending with the word 'you' but it does not feel contrived because France handles the line breaks well and keeps the poem flowing smoothly:

> Count the years it went into hiding and you
> walked down a long road in a body you
>
> couldn't call your own. Every time you
> looked all you could see was bone. You
>
> swallowed a memory of milk ...

France is not always so successful with her couplets; in 'Yes' there is a sense that the poem is being driven by the requirements of the form and the rhymes clunk in places. It might have been better to employ some slant or eye rhymes, and it is fair to say that this concern to stay within the requirements of a restrictive form can sometimes lead to the occasional redundancy. In the final couplet of 'Yes', 'Now I practise *Yes, Do* and *Try*. / Sometimes I fall, but sometimes I can fly' to my ears, that 'can' should have been excised. There are times, too, when France is telling the reader either some homely truths or what to think:

> We all need more courage
> for peace than for war, more lightness of heart
>
>   ('You are Her')

and

> None of us can know how or when
> our death will happen – till then
> we must make our own devotions.

('Last Day')

It is easy enough to pick out such infelicities, but these are minor in the context of the volume taken as a whole. There are many excellent poems here, such as the well structured and carefully balanced 'The Somethingosphere', the powerfully metaphoric 'Bowl' with its '*bowl*, a vessel that will crack / and be mended, crack and be mended', and the evocative 'The Sound of Snipe' with its visionary vignettes: 'A wooden ladder leading nowhere. // An arrow zeroing through air / just before it lands a bullseye'.

A further richness to be found in *You are Her* is the occasional erotic slant given to some of the poems as, for example, in 'No Subject':

> We haven't really agreed upon our object
> and I know it's always a delicate subject
> but let's put it first, try it at least – that verb.

France is too experienced a poet to betray influences, but there are echoes which can enhance a poem; 'What Love is like in Winter' ends with 'what will become of us is stars' which, while recalling Larkin in Arundel, is original and memorable in itself. Sometimes, perhaps surprisingly, there are echoes of Plath:

> It's a plaster vase
> I arrange the stem
> of myself in; it drinks
> sweat, my sins.

('Frida Kahlo's Corset')

But this is glancingly touched, serving only to sharpen our sense of how the poetic tradition continues to make inroads into our metaphoric vocabulary.

Helen Mort

Helen Mort, 24, was born in Sheffield and currently lives in Cumbria where she is Poet in Residence at The Wordsworth Trust. She received an Eric Gregory Award in 2007 and has two pamphlets with Tall-Lighthouse press. One of them, *A Pint for the Ghost*, was a Poetry Book Society Choice for Spring 2010. She is working towards her first full collection.

Heirloom

You will inherit it: this off-white box of cigarettes,
untouched, slipped down the family tree
from man to man. Inside, a sawdust smell,
a regiment of twenty strong, upright,
preserved from damp. More subtle than
a brooch, more portable than silverware.
A token from the time your granddad never
leaned out from the deck of a navy ship
and let his ash vanish into the waves,
a keepsake from the graveyard where
your father never stood at nights
leaning across the wall, blowing
rings out from the living to the dead.
Non-smokers, all of us. You'll keep them,
as we each have, in a cabinet: unopened,
locked. Some nights you'll swear you smell them
through the box, the wooden casing
of the drawer, as if they'd lit themselves
and smouldered there; our history,
burning on its own slight flame.

Claustrophobia

Not the lift doors as they clank into a kiss again;
a house's cellar with its papercut of light; a seat
boxed in by others, empty and identical.
Not an airless cupboard, but a landscape
where you could drive anywhere; a room
in darkness so you have to dream the corners
where a spider might unfurl its origami legs;
a river that reveals your face with all
a mirror's half-apologetic accuracy; a day
of freedom and the mind's own dry stone wall.
The thought of towns you've never visited,
names that never came to you at night.

Hull Cemetery

The morning slips. The afternoon retracts its hand.
A sober graveyard where the headstones hardly stand,
each stately set of tombs a set of leaning shelves,
embarrassments of riches now shaming themselves.

Beer cans. Fag ends. In death, the most aloof of men
give up and let the nettles climb all over them -
the famous mariner lost years ago at sea
his name washed up amongst the blue graffiti,

here at the fringes, where each gothic arch lets go
its purchase, faints into the arms of the hedgerow.
An obelisk points up at nothing but the rain.
The day's collapsed. The night's for building it again.

Common Names

Somewhere, there is a spider called *Harrison Ford,*
another genus known as *Orson Welles.* The ocean's full
of seahorses who take their names from racing champs.
Above our heads, a solitary *Greta Garbo* wasp takes flight.

Each day, someone adopts a killer whale or buys
a patch of moon only to call it *Bob* and last night,
watching meteors sail drunk across the Grasmere sky,
you told me there are minor planets christened

Elvis, Nietzsche, Mr Spock. So forgive me if I looked up
past your face, to see those nearly-silver drops
make rivers in the dark, and, for a moment,
almost thought there might be stars named after us.

Fiona Sampson

The Loneliness of the Autodidact

Poetry Writing: The Expert Guide Fiona Sampson (Robert Hale, 2009)

When Robert Hale talked to me about this project, I knew that I wanted to produce the book I'd needed when I was first writing poetry. Access to poetry-writing is changing, of course. Not only has workshop culture become ubiquitous, but university writing programmes, from undergraduate to doctoral level, make a serious apprenticeship – with the Plan B of a qualification – available to everyone, not just the lucky recipients of circumstantial patronage.

I think it's foolish, though, to assume that no-one emerges by any other route. There will always be talented writers who haven't the money, or time, for formal institutional study. Even more to the point, at that first moment when people – often young, but not necessarily – think of writing, they're *outside* the community that understands how necessary practice – apprenticeship – is. As a reader of *Agenda*, you'll probably feel this is axiomatic: but the broadsheets, and other arts media, still pedal the fantasy that poets are born not made, and that when a new poet comes to the fore they're doing so with the first poems they ever wrote. I remember how guilty I felt when I worked at my own early poems, certain that to do so was self-delusional – that one couldn't *become* good, one must just *be* that way... I simply didn't have anyone to tell me otherwise. I read wonderful poetry, and wrote lousy poetry, and had no bridge between the two. I knew how to *read* a poem – at least at the level of meaning and imagery – but not how to *build* one. I didn't even get the basics of poetic 'grammar' at university, where I'd gone as a mature student in an attempt to find that bridge.

So, having wasted years stumbling about in the autodidactic dark, when Robert Hale said they were looking for a poetry book in their *Expert Guide* series, I knew straight away that I wanted to write a *vade mecum* for my past self. It was my own experience of having to develop without guide or mentor that I believed qualified me for this task. I wanted to encourage: because it seems to me that lack of confidence is a real barrier to good writing. But I didn't want to patronise: when you're eager to write you don't need prompts or games, but methods and knowledge. Formal knowledge isn't elitist: but it *is* elitist to withhold it. A poet can decide for herself whether and how she uses a particular technique – but only once she has it in her armoury.

This kind of knowledge does build methodically: to take an obvious example, work with strict rhyming forms entails the various kinds of rhyme and they, in turn, entail metre. At the same time, to be continually useful a guide must also work as a reference book. So I tried to arrange topics chapter by chapter, *and* in practical order. I interspersed technical with non-technical, practical topics such as what to write about and whether to publish – because I remembered having these questions too. This extract, for example, is from *Chapter 2. Going in: finding and using your material:*

*

Poetry looks both in and outward. My writing table is below a window: in fact, it's surrounded by windows, since I work in a garden shed. Shed and garden are surrounded in turn by fields. These are very much a workplace, just like my shed: agro-industrial plant roll up and down to a nearby drying hanger. The shed walls are thin, and on its flat roof birds' footsteps sound like hooves.

This seems to me a good position to be in. I'm enclosed by – and from – the landscape. I can observe it at some moments and ignore it at others. And that kind of selection is something poetry's particularly good at. In fact we could say that poetry *is* measure: both in the old sense of a musical phrase and in the wider sense that it juxtaposes and allocates, choosing to take so much of one element and a little more of another in order to create a distinctive mixture. To put it another way, poetry measures-out both form and content. This doesn't make it either systematic or predictable. But it does mean that, for the writer, pattern and proportion are part of the trick of it. […]

So what *is* poetic material? It's the internal reality that produces poetry. This isn't simply the life of the emotions (and it's certainly not a set of symptoms: poetry isn't a form of therapy). Nor is it just the unconscious, which we might assume to be rich and incomprehensible but by definition out of reach. Poetic material *is* partly made up of these psychic elements; but it is also includes themes and preoccupations, a world-view and cultural background – and beliefs about poetry. It's the *why* of writing: which produces the *which*.

The poet Peter Redgrove's 'formula' for a true poem asked the writer to use the whole quartet of senses, emotion, intellect and intuition, and is one of the most challenging, and at the same time accurate, definitions of poetry we have. […] Poetry, since it looks both out and in, has to be *about* something in order to be fully present. That doesn't mean it must be intellectually-driven, or politically-engaged, or that its meaning is somewhere beyond the poem itself, in a cultural situation or emotional climate which verse helps us to understand. But it does mean that the poem is *exploring something*: even if that 'something' is simply its own form, as is the case with such famous poetic games-players as Gertrude Stein or the automatic-writing Surrealists. Contrary to popular belief, poems very rarely do nothing except describe a 'sweet, especial rural scene', as Gerard Manley Hopkins's 'Binsey Poplars' has it. William Wordsworth's 'Daffodils', one of the most-traduced poems in the English Romantic tradition, is in fact about the nature of experience: about *what it is like to remember* his 'host of golden daffodils', how 'They flash upon the inward eye / That is the bliss of solitude'. And even descriptive poetry is always more than a mere record. A poem is never a holiday snap. Instead, poetic material is a mixture of emotion, observation, insight, preoccupation... It is, in short, a mixture of elements very much like the self who writes. [...]

Peter Redgrove's cross-roads of forces reminds us how the full range of who you are must be brought to bear in poetry. After all, if a poem is, as T.S.Eliot says in 'East Coker', a 'raid on the inarticulate' – if it is at all mysterious, going further than what we think we know – it certainly can't know *less* than its author. A good poem is more than the sum of its own parts: and must be more than the sum of the poet's parts too. [...] Writing poetry is *not*, despite the way some opportunities for participation seem to have been put together, a competition. Instead, it means being in a particular relationship to your *own* capacities. [...] In his famous definition of Negative Capability, from a letter to his brothers in 1817, John Keats talks about the poet as 'capable of being in uncertainties, Mysteries, doubts without any irritable reaching after fact & reason'. Yet he wasn't advocating writerly indecision but, rather, a profound openness to possibilities that might occur within the writing process. To begin with – to create the habit – it may help to think of this in more active terms. The starting point for a poem must be a place where *everything* is thinkable. There can be no thought police at the source of writing. [...]

Poets devise many ways of accessing the full range of their own material. All are strategies for getting round the internal censors. [...] Seamus Heaney digs down *from where he is* to find his own layers of meaning and resonance. He aspires to be workmanlike, immediate, and concrete. 'But I've no spade to follow men like them', he says of his farming family, in 'Digging'. These poems ask their speaker, *Who are you?* and, in starting from where he is, they are profoundly reflexive. [...] For Ted Hughes on the other hand, the great effort is to get beyond the self to the given world. [...] Hughes's essay 'The Burnt Fox', tells us how the incidents in his famous poem 'The Thought Fox' really happened: the idea for the poem seemed to 'enter' the poet's mind because he made himself open to it.

How to make yourself open like this? Poetry requires wool-gathering;

the kind of unfocused browsing and pottering which so irritates the people we live with. The poet doesn't know *what* she's looking for as she reads a couple of poems in a magazine, glances at the newspaper, wanders round the room picking things up and putting them down again. The metabolism of consciousness is mysterious. It is by nature prior to, and hidden from, the content of thought. Once you start to think, *I'm creatively wool-gathering*, your attention switches to yourself, you become self-conscious and the process stops. So this deliberate entry into a more spacious way of thinking has to get past self-consciousness […] the censors who stand at the gates of your consciousness telling you, for example, *You've nothing interesting to say. No-one's going to read this. No thought but in rhyme. Watch your language*, or best of all, *So-and-so doesn't do it like this.* […]

One way to stop self-sabotage is to write poems 'in dialogue with' work you admire. […] It's a bit like wearing a mask. It's also a bit like avoiding shyness, in a room where you know no-one, by asking someone *else* about themselves. Some writers use music, when they're writing, to set the tone of what they want to write *and* to occupy part of their attention. Music, after all, is a human language and it's almost impossible not to 'follow' it. […] Some people write in cafés or other public places, where the 'white noise' of outer life can be enough to prevent self-consciousness. […] One of the most persuasive advocates of the café writing table is Natalie Goldberg, whose inspirational *Writing Down the Bones* is built on the importance of free writing – of 'going in' – as a *practice*, a repeated discipline. […] Some writers go further still with the threshold of consciousness. They practice forms of self-hypnosis. The poet Herbert Lomas lies on a sofa and talks himself down seven flights of imaginary stairs, along a visualised corridor and into the furthest room, where he lies down on a sofa and writes a poem. It's a technique he developed while he was teaching full time and had so little time to write that he had to make what was available work. […]

Going in to your poetic material is a way to get closer to your *own* self, rather than the self who has written so far, or a version of you constructed by the people around you. At the same time it's an adventure, in which you go beyond external aspects in order to catch up with another, less familiar, version of your own self. Poetry is always on the edge of stepping out into what you don't know: into a self you don't recognise, beyond the rational and comprehensible into more archaic forms of knowledge. Beyond this threshold are shapes that aren't yet recognisable: they might be encouraging or terrifying. Your job is to observe them without getting carried away from the lighted room you need to write in. Poets, like poetry, look both ways.

Notes on contributors

Gary Allen was born in Ballymena, Co. Antrim. He has been widely published in magazines, including, *Ambit, Antigonish Review, Edinburgh Review, Irish Pages, London Magazine, Poetry Ireland Review, Poetry New Zealand, The Poetry Review, South Carolina Review, Stand, The Yellow Nib. Iscariot's Dream* was published by Agenda Editions in 2008. A tenth collection, *Ha, Ha,* is due this autumn from Lagan Press. A selection of his poems was included in the anthology, *The New North*, Wake Forest University Press, North Carolina. He recently received an award from the Arts Council of Northern Ireland.

Joseph Allen was born in Ballymena, Co. Antrim, Nr. Ireland. He has been published in various magazines, including *Acumen, Antigonish Review, Cyphers, London Magazine, Orbis, Poetry Ireland Review, Red Wheelbarrow, The Reader, Ropes, South Carolina Review, Poetry Salzburg Review, the Shop*. Four collections of his poetry have been published, the most recent being *Family Plot*, Lagan Press, 2008. A new collection, *Looking for Robert Johnson*, is due from Lagan Press, 2011. He recently received an award from the Arts Council of Northern Ireland.

Fred Beake has been active as a poet, editor (the Poet's Voice and Mammon Press), critic and translator for forty years. He holds a Classics degree from Bristol University and also studied Afro Asian Studies at Sussex University. His published translations range from Robert Desnos' long surrealist poem *The Night of Loveless Nights* to Aristophanes' *Peace*. His *New and Selected Poems* was published by Shearsman in 2005. A new volume is due from Shoestring in 2011. Global Oriental have just published his joint translation (with Ravil Bukharaev) of Kol Gali's medieval Muslim epic, *The Story of Joseph*.

Alison Brackenbury's seventh collection is *Singing in the Dark*, Carcanet, 2008. 'A quiet lyricism and delight' (*The Guardian*). She has recently produced a chapbook of new animal poems, *Shadow*, available from www.happenstancepress.com New poems can be read at her website: www.alisonbrackenbury.co.uk

Lucinda Carey is a member of The Plymouth Language Club and reads regularly at the Callander Poetry Festival. Her work has appeared in various magazines including *Poetry Scotland, Poetry Salzburg* and *THE SHOp*.

Terese Coe's translations have recently appeared in *Agenda, The Times Literary Supplement, Poetry* an in many other journals in the U.S. and the U.K. Her first collection of poems, *The Everyday Uncommon*, won a Wore Press publication prize in 2005.

Belinda Cooke completed her PhD on Robert Lowell's interest in Osip Mandelstam in 1993. She has published three books to date: *Resting Place* (Flarestack Publishing, 2008); *The Paths of the Beggarwoman: Selected Poems of Marina Tsvetaeva*, (Worple Press, 2008) and (in collaboration with Richard McKane) *Flags* by Boris Poplavsky, (Shearsman Press, 2009). She and Richard also have a collection of Boris Pasternak's later poems forthcoming.

David Cooke was born in Wokingham in 1953 of Irish parents. He won a Gregory Award in 1977 and has published poems and reviews in both the UK and Ireland. After a long absence he has started writing again. His new collection *In The Distance* will be forthcoming from Night Publishing early next year.

John F. Deane was born on Achill Island in 1943. He founded *Poetry Ireland* – the National Poetry Society – and *The Poetry Ireland Review*. He has won the O'Shaughnessy Award for Irish Poetry, and the Marten Toonder Award for Literature and poetry prizes from Italy and Romania. He has been shortlisted for both the T.S. Eliot prize and The Irish Times Poetry Now Award, and has won residencies in Bavaria, Monaco and Paris. His poetry collection, *The Instruments of Art*, came from Carcanet in 2005, *In Dogged Loyalty*, essays on religious poetry, Columba 2006, and *From The Marrow-Bone*, also from Columba, 2008. His latest poetry collection is *A Little Book of Hours*, Carcanet 2008. He is a member of Aosdána. In 2007 the French Government honoured him by making him Chevalier de l'ordre des arts et des lettres. In 2008 he was visiting scholar in the Burns Library of Boston College. Later this year Columba Press will publish a book of essays, *The Works of Love*. His next poetry collection, *Eye of the Hare*, will come from Carcanet in June 2011.

Felix Dennis began writing poetry after a life-threatening illness, and authored his first book of verse, *A Glass Half Full*, in 2002. His *Did I mention the Free Wine?* poetry tours have entertained thousands of poetry-lovers, as well as those not usually drawn to poetry, on both sides of the Atlantic. His poetry has been regularly featured on radio programmes. His poetry collections include *Homeless in My Heart, A Glass Half Full, Lone Wolf, Nursery Rhymes for Modern Times* and *Island of Dreams*. His latest book of verse, *Tales from the Woods,* has just been launched.

Angela France has completed an MA in Creative and Critical Writing at the University of Gloucestershire, and is now studying for a PhD. Her second collection, *Occupation*, was published last year by Ragged Raven Press. She is features editor of *Iota*.

John Freeman lives in the Vale of Glamorgan and teaches at Cardiff University. His most recent collection is *A Suite for Summer* (Worple Press, Tonbridge, 2007).

John Gladwell was born in Lincoln and now lives on the North Essex coast where he teaches part time in adult education. He has previously had work published in a variety of magazines including *PN Review, Stand, Ambit, The Rialto, Staple* and *The Reader*.

Alyson Hallett's latest collection of poems is *The Stone Library* (Peterloo Poets). She has just completed a practice-based PhD in poetry and is currently poet-in-residence in Exeter University's Geography Department on the Tremough Campus, Falmouth.

Fawzia Kane was born in San Fernando, Trinidad, and came to the UK on a scholarship to study architecture. She now lives and practises as an architect in London. She began writing poems in earnest around ten years ago after attending Arvon and Poetry School courses. Her work has been published in several magazines, including *Poetry Wales, Poetry London, the Rialto, the Shop* and the *Interpreter's House*. In 2003, she was one of the featured poets of the Poetry School anthology, *Entering the Tapestry* (Enitharmon).

Tim Liardet has produced six full collections of poetry. *The Blood Choir*, his fifth collection, won an Arts Council of England Writer's Award as a collection-in-progress in 2003, was a Poetry Book Society Recommendation for Summer 2006 and shortlisted for the 2006 T S Eliot Prize. His chapbook – *Priest Skear* (reviewed here) – appeared this year; *The Storm House*, his sixth full collection, is due from Carcanet in 2011. He is Professor of Poetry at Bath Spa University.

Christopher Locke's poems have appeared or are forthcoming in such magazines as *Southwest Review*, *The Literary Review, Contemporary American Voices, The Sun, Agenda, Tears in the Fence, Descant* (Canada), and *The Stinging Fly* (Ireland). He has published four chapbooks of poetry. His first full length collection of poems, *End of American Magic*, was recently released (Salmon Poetry, 2010). Chris lives in New Lebanon, NY with his wife and two daughters and teaches literature and writing at The Darrow School.

Christine McNeill's third collection will be published by *Shoestring Press* in 2011. She is currently working on a new one on the theme of music and Austrian composers.

Andrew McNeillie's most recent book of poems, *In Mortal Memory* (reviewed by Patricia McCarthy in *The Warwick Review*) was published this year by Carcanet Press. His memoir, *Once*, came out in 2009. He is Professor of English at Exeter University.

Kathy Miles was born in Liverpool and moved to Wales in 1972. She now works in the Learning Resources Centre at the University of Wales. She has produced three poetry collections, the latest of which, *The Shadow-House*, was published by Cinnamon Press in 2009. A poem of hers was chosen to appear in the 2008 Forward Book of Poetry. She lives near Aberaeron, and was made a full member of the Welsh Academi in 2009.

W S Milne is an Aberdeen poet living in Surrey. His books of poems include *Twa-Three Lines* and *Sangs o Luve and Pairtan*. He has published a critical monograph on the poetry of Geoffrey Hill, and has recently made a programme on *The Waste Land* with Joan Bakewell for BBC Radio 4.

Lyn Moir, born in Scotland in 1934**,** has published collections with Arrowhead in 2001 and 2003. Calder Wood Press published *Easterly, Force 10* in 2009 and will publish her fourth, *Velázquez's Riddle*, early in 2011. She lives in St. Andrews, on the harbour.

Jean O'Brien's third collection of poetry, *Lovely Legs*, came out from Salmon Publishing in 2009. She is currently working on a new collection. Her work is widely published, anthologised and broadcast in Ireland and elsewhere. She has taught Creative Writing in The Irish Writers Centre for the past ten years. She is the featured poet in the current *New Hibernian Review*, USA.

Thomas O'Grady teaches Irish Literature and Creative Writing at the University of Massachusetts. He also plays the guitar in a jazz combo. His first collection, *What Really Matters,* was published in 2000 by McGill-Queens University Press. Another collection of poems is on its way.

Tony Roberts was educated in England and America. He has published three poetry collections: *Flowers of the Hudson Bay* (Peterloo), *Sitters* (Arc) and, in 2010, *Outsiders* (Shoestring Press). His poems, reviews and essays appear regularly in the literary press.

Sue Roe's poetry has appeared in *New Poetries III* (Carcanet) as well as in literary journals including *Agenda*, *New Writing*, *New Poetry Quarterly*, *Paintbrush* and *the Rialto*. Sue is author of *The Private Lives of the Impressionists* (Vintage (UK) and HarperCollins (US)), which is translated into six languages, and of *Gwen John: A Life* (Vintage (UK) and Farrar, Straus & Giroux (US)). She also works with contemporary artists including Corinna Button, Marco Crivello and Anne Penman Sweet, writing exhibition catalogues for galleries in London and elsewhere. She is Senior Lecturer in Creative Studies at the University of Sussex, where she teaches creative writing and runs the MA in Creative Writing & Authorship. She lives in Brighton.

Julie-ann Rowell's pamphlet collection *Convergence* was selected as a recommended read by the Poetry Book Society. Her first full collection, *Letters North* was published in 2008 by Brodie Press. She has won several prizes and commendations, and teaches creative writing in Bristol.

Fiona Sampson has published seventeen books, most recently *Rough Music* (shortlisted for the 2010 Forward Prize for best collection), *Poetry Writing* (2009) and *A Century of Poetry Review* (PBS Special Commendation, 2009), with ten in translation. She has been awarded the Newdigate Prize, been short-listed for Forward single-poem and T.S. Eliot prize, received a Cholmondeley Award and is an FRSL. Forthcoming in spring 2011 are the Newcastle/Bloodaxe Poetry Lectures, and Faber Poet-to-poet, *Shelley*.

Rosie Shepperd is currently studying for a postgraduate degree (poetry) at Glamorgan University. Her poems have appeared in *Poetry London*, *Poetry Ireland*, *Poetry Wales*, *Rialto*. She was one of six finalists for the 2008 Manchester Poetry Prize and last year she won the Ted Walters/Liverpool University Prize.

James Simpson was a prizewinner in the Thomas Hardy Society's James Gibson Memorial Poetry Competition. He has recently collaborated with the artist and printmaker Carolyn Trant on an artist's book, *Hunting the Wren* (Parvenu / Actaeon Press).

Alex Smith was brought up in East London and Essex and now lives in Saffron Walden on the Essex-Cambridgeshire border. He studied economics and finance at what is now the London Metropolitan University and had a successful career in banking. He has had three full collections published. In 2001 he gained an M.Phil in creative writing at Glamorgan University and went on to teach creative writing at Cambridge Regional College and for the Lifelong Learning Programme at Essex University. His work has appeared in a wide range of poetry magazines and journals. He currently reviews for *Poetry Review*. His most recent poetry collection is *Venetian Blue* (Dark Age Press, 2010).

Visit the website

TEAR–OFF SUBSCRIPTION FORM

Pay by cheque (payable to 'Agenda'), or
Visa / MasterCard

SUBSCRIPTION RATES ON INSIDE FRONT COVER

1 Subscription (1 year) =

> 2 double issues
> 1 double, 2 single issues
> or
> 4 single issues
> (The above is variable)

Please print

Name: ....

Address: ....

....

....

.... Postcode ....

Tel: ....

Email: ....

Visa / MasterCard No: ☐☐☐☐ – ☐☐☐☐ – ☐☐☐☐ – ☐☐☐☐

Expiry date: ☐☐ – ☐☐

Please tick box:

New Subscription ☐   Renewed Subscription ☐

(or subscribe online – www.agendapoetry.co.uk)

Send to: AGENDA, The Wheelwrights, Fletching Street, Mayfield,
East Sussex, TN20 6TL
Tel: 01435-873703